Jane's Stories II: An Anthology by Midwestern Women

Edited by
Glenda Bailey-Mershon

Wild Dove

Studio and Press, Inc.
Palatine, Illinois

Published by
Wild Dove Studio and Press, Inc., P.O. Box 789, Palatine, Illinois 60078-0789

Library of Congress Catalog Card Number: 99-75798
Jane's Stories II: An Anthology by Midwestern Women/Edited by Glenda Bailey-Mershon.

ISBN 0-9639894-3-X

Cover design by Annette Bliudzius and Glenda Bailey-Mershon
Printed and bound in the United States of America

CONTENTS

Note from the Editor

Wild Dove has a dual mission to promote writing that is centerd in women's experiences and in regional identity. *Jane's Stories II*, like the original *Jane's Stories*, enables us to fulfill both parts of our mission by bringing to you a collection of women writers whose work reveals both the female and the Midwesterner. We are particularly pleased to bring to you so many new voices.

Emerging writers join seasoned writers in this volume. Here you will find Alice Friman, winner of the 1998 Ezra Pound Poetry Award; several who have been nominees or winners of the Pushcart Prize, including Marilyn Krysl, Tamara Sellman, Marjorie Maddox, and Sandra Sidman Larson; and Lambda Award finalist Jess Wells. Some contributors have achieved other marks of literary distinction: Yaddo, McDowell, Ragdale and Norcroft residencies, NEA fellows, and more.

But we think readers will be just as delighted by the voices of newcomers. Late bloomers, busy mothers, and even one high school student have brought exciting work to this volume.

As for regional interests, the selections for this edition were made without knowledge of the authors' identities; thus, we cannot claim to present a blend of Midwestern women's voices that is balanced by geography, any more than it is by ethnicity, religion, or other important social attributes. However, our submission criteria noted our interest in regional writing as well as our commitment to diversity, and, consequently, we present a panoply of views and backgrounds that reflects an inclusive vision of the Midwestern identity, and which covers well the geographical territory.

Nor do we claim to present a selection that invokes any particular theory about Midwestern cultural identity. Yet we will note with reference to Scott Russell Sanders' work on this point, that the theme of escape from constraints is often married in these stories, poems, and essays with a genuine love and sense of protection for the natural world of field, stream, farm, and forest. Even satisfaction in the urban terrain is found here in stories such as Roz Warren's "Auto Repair," set in the Motor City of Detroit, and Gayle Brandeis' "Sugar Rush," with its analogies spun from Chicago's skyline. And when Marjorie Maddox invokes memories of a family traveling by car through the Ohio countryside to the tunes of the parents' courtship, or the reader meditates with Mary Ber on the consolation to be found in a suburban garden, we touch for a moment the nexus between place and insight.

In any case, we at Wild Dove feel satisfied that we have achieved our goal of presenting to readers a selection of work that is at once woman-centered and Midwestern in setting and influence. We look forward to sharing these works with you, and to hearing your response to them. Please join us for the readings, discussions, and workshops which will take place across the country as we present to the public this latest evidence of the Midwestern wealth in writers.

Glenda Bailey-Mershon
Palatine, Illinois
October, 1999

Acknowledgements and Dedication

This edition of *Jane's Stories* is the product of many women working together to advance a common vision of woman-centered writing and publishing. The editor wishes to thank for their assistance the *Jane's Stories* Editorial Board: Linda Mowry, Julie Sass, and Clara Johnson, who read and evaluated hundreds of manuscripts. In the production and promotion stages, the Editorial Board was joined by Jan Kent and (after their work was selected for inclusion) by Ridgely Jackson, Christine Swanberg, Shobha Sharma, and Linda Mitchell, whose assistance with proofreading, layout and design, promotion, and communications was invaluable. Together with the Editorial Board and myself, all of these women make up the *Jane's Stories II* Cooperative.

We dedicate this volume to the women-in-print movement, to all the writers, publishers, booksellers, agents and readers who work for the inclusion of women's voices in our culture, and to all the voices yet to be heard.

Poetry

Alice Friman

LETTER TO THE CHILDREN

In the new cold of late September
the prongs of Queen Anne's lace that held
their doilies up like jewels
rise then stiffen, crushing toward center,
making wooden enclosures to die in
like the ones the Celts built to hold their enemies
then set aflame. The goldenrod leans,
licks at their cages. And all that's left of daisies
are burnt out eyes.

I walk these back fields
past the swish of cattails in their silver
grasses, the old ones
showing the woolly lining of their suede jackets
while the thistle, dried to gray,
bends her trembling head
and spills her seed.

It is the time—the great lying-in of Autumn—
and I am walking its wards.
And I remember it was now, late September
then on into the deep gully of fall—when the hackberry
groans and the black oak strains in its sockets, the winds
pushing in the long forest corridors—
that I too was born and gave birth.

And you are all Autumn's children, all
given to sadness amid great stirrings
for you were rocked to sleep in the knowledge
of loss and saw in the reflection outside your window,
behind the bars of your reach, your own face
beckoning from the burning promise
that little by little disappeared. What can I give you

for your birthdays this year, you who are the match
and the flaming jewel, whose birthright consumes itself
in the face of your desire?

If you were here with me now
walking down this day's death,
I would try to show you two things: how the last light
plays itself out over the thistle's labors,
over the wild cherry heavy with fruit, as if comfort
lay in what it had made. And how that black bird
with flame at his shoulders
teeters for balance on a swaying weed.

TELLING TALES
NEW HARMONY, INDIANA

The 8-legged calf was born the year
Charlie Sloniker came to town.
4 legs in back, 2 in front, and up
from the withers 2 that fell over like
2 braids come down, tucking into
hooves instead of bows. The face wore
3 eyes and 2 mouths, one on each side.
Only the rear was separated—2 tails 2 rumps.
Why, if you saw it from behind, looked like
2 brothers so close they had to graze the
same side of one clover patch for peace.
Sam Bayless and Tommy Lanham showed it
at the fair when Tom's scissors-grinding
slacked off and Sam took time out from
fiddling on Saturday nights. And people
came to see, scratched their middles,
shook their heads—paid too. But Ida
said it was a shame the way they gawked,
said Sam had no right, taking advantage
the way he did and her pregnant and all

and up each night worrying herself, feeling
around, counting pokes and pricks, while Sam
snored to the wall, his fiddling foot
still for once. Must have driven her crazy,
that foot! Could be worse. Take Carolina
next door, saving her own baby coffin box
her people brought over on the boat in case
she turned and died, so delicate she was.
Humph! 190 pounds of delicate and still
setting that box right out so's people could
see it on that cherry side table she had
shipped in first class from St. Louis.
Little oval blue thing. Why, it wasn't
big enough to make a shark's lunch.
Now that calf, that's another thing. Still
it didn't seem right and right after that
nice Mr. Owen died. Of course, he'd been
famous and all but can you imagine drinking
a whole glass of embalming fluid by mistake
instead of the medicated waters Mr. Fretageot
the pharmacist fixed up for him every night?
Of course he had two wives, Mr. Owen did.
But after all, it *was* Mr. Owen and you'd
have to say he was different—collecting
rocks, doing surveys and who knows what all
for the government. Ida used to remark
the letters and packages that man gets,
he'll make this town famous yet. Remarried
he did, remember? Old man Neef's daughter,
Anne Elizabeth. The end of March I think
it was, daffodils out already and she in white
silk slippers, laced all pretty up the sides.

I don't know, seems like nothing
happens much around here but then
looking back it all squeezes down.
Ida, she says she has funny dreams about

things, being pregnant again and all,
but I tell her not to worry. You can't
tell what lasts or counts in this world.
Maybe that stuffed calf and Carolina's
blue baby box will end up in a museum some
day with Anne Elizabeth's tiny shoes
and Mr. Owen's mail. We both have a good
laugh at that, sipping tea in Ida's yard
out back by the azaleas.

Jennifer Armstrong

STREET SINGING IN CHICAGO IN JANUARY

My feet are no longer feet
they are the ice-bound extensions of this subway platform
to which I am attached
My fingers are no longer flesh
they are chiseled from solid ice
Four slender arcs carved above the strings of the violin
My ears are too numb to mind the roar of the trains
through this dark, unfeeling, subway tomb
My music died an hour past
The bow shovels up the notes and heaves them in icy chunks
to the track below, where the trains shatter them in passing
My musical offering lies in glittering defeat
on the mounds of dirty snow
No nod, no smile, no look has come my way
No coins have found a home in the hopeful hat
No one says, "Yes, we hear you and it is good."
Perhaps I'm dead
but no...
No coins stop my eyes
They see clearly down the long black tunnel stretching out before me
No! This couldn't be my path. I must have taken a wrong turning
I refuse this bleak journey
I'm not asking for much
I'm not crying for thunderous applause at Carnegie Hall
I'm talking about now
Right now
all I need is a smile
and a hot bowl of soup

Susan Marie Scavo

ON MY RELIGIOUS UPBRINGING

What I remember is that bike.
A simple frame of red metal,
ten speeds. The sound
of thin tires on hard concrete.
Handles curving for palms.

What I remember is forgetting
boundaries of flesh and metal. Steering
without hands, maneuvering
with fresh muscle. The wholeness
of body and bike taking corners.

What I remember is dividing waves
of air, a hymn of wind tuned
only for my ears. Leaning into motion,
everything dissolving but that wind, that
endless asphalt. The humming of cells.

What I remember
are those long hours
alone
when no one could
keep up with me.

Diane Lutovich

NOSOUND

Sunday afternoons on Elm Avenue, nosound
throbs like the second before orgasm.

Once it was the nosound of a Minnesota afternoon
on the eve of VJ Day, air wrapped trees,
stifled birds; summer heat stuck to cement, between
fingers. On Sixth Avenue, only ghosts of cars moved;
real ones, stripped of rubber and oil,
rested on blocks.

In those days, I moved through space
as if it were cream; my father could vaporize,
the spaniel rolled its whimpers
into black fur,
we heard the sun set.

Now, when nosound shrouds my street
where cats usually caterwaul and cars and dogs groan,

my skin tightens,
hands become ears.

It is the nosound of my daughter's room,
abandoned on her way to life leaving
outgrown socks,
unmatched shoes.

Of the moments after the dead are covered with dirt
and mourners have returned to their homes;

the nosound of blackberries thickening,
my father's grave;

the nosound of an empty sky after
green and gold shards, left by the last firework
turned into stars.

Ann Darr

THE BAGLEY IOWA POEM

1.

Bagley meant to be
a railroad town
but the railroad
hadn't heard.

Three churches
poulticed
600 people
(five ninety-nine
after I ran away.)

The sneaky holy-roller summer—
with Christian Endeavor
serving as the dating bureau—
on Main street sat the Methodist madam.

God's sparrow
never flew in our trees
and the angling birch
filling my window
turned into a creaking skeleton
when I became
homesick at home.

2.

No was a great big
thousand letter word
and the consequences
were plenty.

Yes was love
and all that
meant, soured
and scourged
with unhappy knots
that tied the men
to their women
and the women
to their men
and the land
heaved and buckled
and produced
2¢ a bushel
          corn
and separate rooms.

3.

Bagley,
well, yes,
heaved on winter streets,
sweltered in the summer.
Grandma Plummer,
deaf as a post
hole,
traded the attic
for a double-carpeted
dining room
two husbands later.
I don't think I
was through with weddings
before I began but
the illustrations
were out of focus
and the hills
were full of accidents
and proposals.

4.

I fly back to my childhood
trying to get the water-tower
shape right. Shaped like a—

I sneak up on it through the trees,
the apple trees that are young
and shapely. Shaped like —

There on its long spindly legs,
the fat tub of a water-tower
towers over the splattered town

shaped like a great bruise
with the welts running like
mainstreet and over it the water tower

shaped like a Roman candle
waiting to go off if only
someone would set a match to it.

I bring my torch. Water
tower shaped like Canaveral.
Over and over I have dreamed
of seeing Bagley from the moon.

5.

Learning that the town has no more trains
                    or buses
shouldn't matter to me who will never go there
                    again but
it has put me standing on a corner
under the bus stop sign
in my new graduation suit
and a hat with a flowing scarf

of a color I can't remember
but the dust is blowing—
gum wrappers mince down the street
making their small journey—
and I am headed away.

Deanna Blackwell

EMANCIPATION

my hair
falls
to the floor
like shackles
to the ground
hand rubs
curiously against
ripe fuzz
liberation
begins
again

and I know
that just because
I feel free
you may not
be happy
for me

just because
I feel free
that you may
not see
the beauty
in my brave
act against
a society
that tells me
to be skinny
    be white
            long hair
            bare there
                        be anyone

but black
but bald
but me.

Marianne Marchese

COFFEE

Listen to me. I mean really listen to me.
Not like you listen to your father.
And don't tune me out like you do your boyfriend.

I'll never understand how you two ended up together anyway.
I mean do you guys even talk, or do you just have sex.
Explain something to me. I heard gay men don't really date.
They just meet and have sex. Is that true?
God you are so lucky!

I wish it was that way for women.
But no. We meet and have to go for coffee.
Coffee....Even before a real date we meet and go for coffee.

I didn't even like coffee till I moved to Chicago.
No wonder Chicago has a coffee house on every corner.
It's for the women!

And coffee is so complicated now.
Short, Tall, Grande, Latte, Foam, No foam
Shit I just want to get laid.

Wait, stop, rewind. We are not supposed to be talking about coffee.
You are supposed to be listening to me and my problem.
Seriously, I just can't believe it's really over.

I honestly thought *this* was the one,
this was the *one*, maybe this *was* the one, and I blew it.
I don't understand why all my relationships end this
way.
Do you think it's me?
Na, it must be the coffee.

Linda Mitchell

BE WILD!
For Marin

Be wild!
Fly the clouds like kites
Fling yourself about like seed
Winnow yourself in air like chaff.

Be wild!
Grow purple flowers in your dining room
Raise dragon flies for pets
Place yourself on rooftops
And call to the herons on the river.

Be wild!
Play your music too loud
Argue intensely in whispers
Light firecrackers for breakfast

Be wild!
Make your hair blue
Play the harmonica at 4:00 am
Dance on every sidewalk you cross.

Be wild!
Call out Yih Hi!
Yip yip yip and yahoo!
And give everyone lip
Everyone!

Be wild!
Watch the burning blue sky till it turns golden
Fall on your face in clover
Be wild! Be won over!

KEYNOTE SPEAKER

Mundelein College
Women's Conference March 1994

Her hands
rest on either edge of the podium.
Leaning on it slightly
her hands touch
not rubbed wood warm to the eye
but instead a cloth to cover it;
a rainbow striped cloth
the color of eyes, skies,
skin and blossom.
The sun shines from it.
The blood of ancestors runs out of it.

She lifts her hand
gesturing a word, releasing a concept
and her hand
falls back to the cloth
lays flat to it
and she rubs it palm flat
she rubs her whole hand
over the cloth
texturing her flesh
with the weave.
She reaches to pat her hair—
adjusts her glasses
scratches her cheek
catches her notion
and her hand falls back to the cloth,
lays flat to it
smooths it
touches in its texture
the women who wove it,
women who made lives for themselves
in the weaving,

women who put their long history
to the test,
put their heads and hands together,
hands folded in prayer,
hands held palms up to heaven
wondering what will come next;
the many hands that toiled
and grew the cotton in the soil
and wove the cotton into community
sustaining community,
sustaining families, themselves;
hands that wove sun the blood
the skin and flower into stripes
weaving their lives past poverty and
starvation into survival.

She speaks worlds of change and struggle
and rubs her hands over the cover.
She speaks worlds of joy and struggle
and rubs her hands over the cover of survival;
rainbow hued brilliance
absorbing the sun
the skin colored
eye colored
flowering past survival
to Life!

Danice Kern

BOILED MOLECULES

We sit steeping in a bathtub,
my little boy and me, like a steaming
pot of tea.

Loosened by fever and fearing,
he puddles his words in breathy, gulping gasps.
Bogey men

lurk in shadows thrown by a faint flame
from a candle on the sink. We chase them
gone with dares.

His hot flesh against mine, we soak,
capturing with our hands and mouths
streamed star stuff:

galaxies from the shower rain.

Our sun, the moon, the stars
and you, he whispers,
these are good.

Gravely, he confides this, my small boy,
smelling suddenly of birth wetness,
sweetly moist and so fragilely washed.

Tell me about the baby stars, Momma.
So I say:

They are made like you,
from the stuff sluicing from this faucet,
the sea,

***

one by one,
from things tinier than bits of loose tea.

We cuddle in our tub of atoms,
like molecules boiled in a fired china pot,
bits of me
my boy, sunbeams, fudge sundaes
and frog bellies, forged in the core
of a star.

My son, think of it.
A furnace hotter than you.

And he laughs.

BEFORE THE POETRY

You did not exist yet on paper

before the poetry
back when the words pushed out of me
still-born in upper and lower case.

Still, I loved the idea of you

before the poetry
back when my words sang to deaf lips
but earnestly and self-taught.

Then, I dressed you in frank verbs and a drab coat.
I measured your cadence and brown whiskers.
You hexed me with your hands and by syllables,

we began to rhyme.

Victoria Dal Compo

GRANDMOTHER'S PORCH

I love my grandmother's porch
It holds pots of basil and peppermint plants, as well as upturned barrels . . .
        and boxes lying about
Wisps of mostaccioli and tomato sauce smells seep through the
                                                        screen door
Behind a faded blue chair I wait until the faint murmurs of my parents and
                                                        aunts and
                                                        uncles

        Stop as the metal door slams shut
I creep out and sit on the chair staring up at the sky with glittering stars
    shining on and off, on and off
Until the call of my mother cuts through my thoughts saying "Dinner time!"
I love my grandmother's porch
It has the comfort of the sun as its robe
    and the smells of basil as its breath

Catherine Mellett

ON THE WAY TO THE RINK

Snow is falling
a beach of white sand on the street
she has always known.
With her pink skates slung over her shoulder
and a quarter for hot chocolate in her mitten
she is queen of the world.
She watches the snow and wonders
what it knows about her.
What it knows is this:
all the details of her first kiss,
the number of times she fell,
the precise moment at which
she'll have to practice the turn
again and again.
It does not know
that this is the last snowfall of the season
or that some day our girl
will stand at her front door
and watch her daughter walk away.
Or that in the watching
she will remember this truant night
and want it back.
More than the candy pink skates.
More than the lessons.

CHILDREN CHASING FIREFLIES AT DUSK

We mean no harm.
What we want is simple.
You can have the pretty black line
like a racing stripe.

Or those things that look like ears.
Or the tiny feet
like an army of commas
in the palm of a hand.

We want what everyone else wants
and are not afraid to chase it.
We want that thing they carry:
We want the light. We want the light.
We want the light.

Andrea Potos

YAYA'S PANTRY

This was before the time of sleek,
faceless cupboards.
This was a world you could walk into,
parting the long thin drape sprigged with yellow flowers,
to rows and rows
of thickly-painted cream-colored drawers, shelves filled
with plump bags of flour, cornmeal, sugar;
jars of sesame seeds, poppy seeds,
the Greek macaroni we called *manestra*,
shimmering gold canisters of olive oil
beside the everyday Wesson.

There, it was easy to stand as still
as you were supposed to in church.
You inhaled the faint aroma of her anise,
her amber-dark bottles of real vanilla
placed alongside cake pans, bread pans, glass mixing bowls
fit together like nesting dolls.
You had to stand on tiptoe and arch your neck
to peer at the highest shelves where she stored her
Jordan almonds and chocolate drops.
Though you could not grasp them, you did not worry,
you knew sooner or later
all her sustenance would reach you.

Shirley Vogler Meister

HARVEST

With gusto, she plunged her hands
into pumpkin pulp, pulling
and scooping until the innards
and seeds slipped loose, and juice
ran down her arms in yellow trickles:
she didn't know she was purging pain.

Watching his wife, he finally felt
the scraping and cutting—the wounds
of the flesh—as if they were his own;
three decades of floods and droughts
on the grounds of marriage come
to harvest in a Hoosier heart
distracted by family pressures.

Newly-made bread and apple butter,
haybarns warmed by cattle breath,
farmwork under a waning sun,
tall purple phlox faded into fall,
pumpkin pies cooling on Halloween—
keen sensations blend into panic
and urgency, like the need to secure
the livestock before a blizzard hits.

Too late...too tired! Emotions sleep
like fallow fields, yearning for new
springs, new dreams: winter follows
autumn, and the pungent pumpkin
is frozen in plastic, waiting.

Shoshauna Shy

WHEN A WISCONSIN SUMMER LASTS INTO OCTOBER

we become unsettled
by dawn licking clouds pink
day after day
We grow suspicious
of velveteen breezes
allowing linens to flap
forgotten on the line
without having to suffer
the punish of rain,
of the crickets' continuous
clicking staccato
oiled by humidity,
uncrushed by frost.

Here in the land of
        don't-put-off-till-tomorrow-what
        a-stitch-in-time-saves
        the-early-bird-gets-the
we find we're seduced little by little
into walking barefoot
half-hungry for breakfast
down to the boathouse
carrying nothing.
Next we are sleeping
in our cotton skivvies
here in the land of
        gotta-work-to-deserve-it
sticking our tongues out
and ducking under fences
mischievous as if
a perpetual childhood
had been wrangled
        and won
from the stars

Christine Swanberg

FOR LEE, WHO SHOES HORSES

I think I could turn, and live with animals,....

Walt Whitman

As you scraped my mare's hoof
then pared its rim so perfectly
it fell like apple rind on hard ground,
I saw suddenly that it's you, Lee,

who keeps me here this October
near the Wisconsin border, winter
starting to nibble lobes, where
the wind's making us a little mean.

It's your *scheeuck-scheeuck-scheeuck*
that keeps me here though I'm tempted
to follow friends to Apple Valley
or Legend Lakes, where there are no

apples, valleys, or legends,
and lakes are stocked with sprinklers.
You keep me from that great shuffle,
the never-paid-for house rumbling

under jets and sunsets so orange
they could be beautiful if you stayed
there long enough. When you came
to curb founder in my horse's feet,

you showed me where the sole was weak.
"We'll put pads on her feet so
the snow won't bite," you said. Just
horsetalk, I know, but wise.

"This mare's a little temperamental,"
you say, and before you nail

the shoes, you rub her withers
   and run your hand so gently past

her fetlocks, she lifts her foot
   like magic. Leaning first, you fold
beneath her shoulder. She drops
   her head to your nape, close enough

to nip you but decides that you're O.K.
   You've culled out a wholeness for her
to stand on, and we both know she's grateful
   for we have a way with animals, don't we?

And Lee, it's just that I live for such kindness.

Morgan Baylog Finn

FARMER'S WIFE IN DEFENSE OF THEIR RUNAWAY TRACTOR

A person could buckle facing the innocence
of buttercups and Queen-Anne's-lace leaning
a breath closer, by dusk, to this land we
prefer barefoot where my Stormy'll pull up

radishes by toe and offer 'em, grinning,
to me as I shoo him off, like a crow,
with my hanky. That man truly thinks nature's
a spunky woman best wooed with humor

and passion if you want buxom summers.
And you know, when sun and rain dance, corn does
billow as it was intended, trailing
sweetness behind us into town. Within

the everlasting determination
of rows, their green-gold unfolding,
I forget all about supper until Stormy
seeks me out by my pink foam rollers,

praising God for a helpmate who rolls from bed
eager to bite into day. And I do,
I do hasten to that rapture most folks call
manure and hay—never forgetting nature's

slyness since our sow grew trough-size from
devouring her young under a cornflower sky;
nature is why our tractor started up by itself
and tore the shed wall, cutting purposefully

through cornfields and night the way Stormy and I
did when we courted. Except we never
zig-zagged two miles, taking down five hundred
feet of fencing, nor did we boomerang off

Ned Maier's stable, leaving his horses
forever bug-eyed, to beach ourselves
atop his new pick-up. (Though, Lord, often
it felt like we had!) "My, doesn't nature

mirror life!" I exclaimed later to Ned.
"Our old tractor thrashing all night
like any decent farmer, aching to run off
for good, but the land pulling stronger."

Marjorie Maddox

CARTOGRAPHY

Simple as a globe spinning
or a quick sketch of the country:
thick black lines as borders,
an ocean here, there,
maybe an interstate running through
and a few rivers, towns.

An entire state scratched on the back of an envelope,
rough, rough draft of an atlas. You trace me like this,
don't expect a dirt path in Kentucky,
freeways wrapped around Chicago, stretched to the East coast;
don't expect veins like roads, heel prints,
boundaries as strong or flimsy as fingernails, as lies.

I'm pinned to place like girders on a bridge,
steel become cold, colder,
like concrete stuck to earth in basements, construction sites.
Sometimes, tugged in and out of coves
in a current too much like a lover,
I float, half-eroded, mouth full of pebbles.

True, the shape of my face is in sand, mountains,
and I sleep to the click of an S.O.S., or not at all.
Because of you, I apply bruises to my cheeks like blush,
to my brow ash from the oldest volcano.
There is more to this than silhouette, than map.

What of your outlines?
An inch into Ohio you pinpoint cities. You're wrong.
This circle is the pond I first made love in,
the dot a patch of poison oak I wore,
a millimeter away: the line where train and Buick
ripped even the sky, severed then from after

while I watched, a car behind.

We draw and redraw maps to keep our footing,
define who and why we are:
thud of fist, jagged cry of a child,
whoosh of water taking in a body—here on paper.
These coastlines are fainter than breath, the barest stencil
of all we want to remember or cannot forget.

OLD TUNES

Oh where have you been, Billy boy, Billy boy?
I have been to seek a wife; she's the joy of my life....

When the road dipped deep
and sky took over the car,
plastering each side of the family 'wagon
with southern Ohio,
and my father's broad grin
caught on the towns of Chillicothe and Portsmouth
while they sucked us in with their steel-mill smoke stacks,
small-town diners, and steeples slanted enough to let
the sun roll down and into the notes
that cluttered the front seat,
we three kids leaned and shoved and grabbed
at my father's songs to make them ours.

Bubbling "Down by the Old Mill Stream,"
we stopped to peel our socks,
wave them at passing trucks,
small prophecies of our victory
as we took the first steps
into the icy wet of his childhood
creek, not once letting go
of the wide hope
of his arm.

And later,
my great aunt's pastry stuck
at the lowest parts of our stomachs,
an awful weight,
we spit out "'Neath the Crust of the Old Apple Pie"
and other melodic jokes
strung on the shaky chords
of my father's voice
from dance halls, summer camps, nights in the navy,
where he dreamed of the slow step
and fingers, smooth as a seductive dance,
that he'd finally find
years later on my mother.

Who was why,
those weeks in the car,
he bellowed and beamed
and zigzagged us into the summers
that smelled and tasted of song:
boogie woogie and be bop, but mostly the cool blue
of Sinatra and Gershwin,
his one hand gliding across the wheel
the other, over and over throughout our lives,
tapping his syncopated love notes
on the open heart of her palm.

Wendy Heller

JUMP ROPE SONG

shame on you
your brother is a monkey
your father is a skunk
your boyfriend is a junkie
your mother is a drunk
shame on you

I am eight years old in the schoolyard
shame on you
no grass, just iron bars
a beach of concrete
flat from far away
up close, duned and many cornered
yet exposed

I am nine years old in the schoolyard
shame on you
in a ring of taunting faces
trying to find shelter
some small piece of me
flies far above, still
I wet my pants

I am ten years old in the schoolyard
shame on you
in an overspill of nipples
from somewhere
I am dumb witness
to the invitation
pinned to my chest

I am eleven years old in the stairwell
shame on you

backed up against the banister
by a sixteen year old boy
shocked hunger eats
emptiness inside me
I don't act
because I am not
with me

I am thirty years old in the schoolyard
shame on me

THE RETURN

The clouds pass,
the rain falls,
and all beings flow into their forms.
(The I Ching)

Before my eyes
a grey squirrel
ran into the middle of Lincoln Avenue
knew its mistake and turned back too late
tumbling under

he was driftwood
in the surf

he was apples
crashing to the ground

he was blades of grass
churning in a mower

I watched him scrabble gravel
alone in his survival, his
single-minded thought to find the tree

implacably out of reach

as a receding
tide, stretching
to fill a footstep

as one edge
of an inch
from the other
as I from the man
in the airport
who suddenly picked up his son
and slammed him
against a post

There won't be any mercy for us
obsessed with the sparkle and tingle
of our lives rushing in
we're oblivious to the ebb
pinned to our heels
until the moon starts reeling it back

driftwood
blades of grass
apples crashing

Y. Regina Whitmore

WORK OF ART

She recalled when there was a special kind
of joy in pain: a calmness and sense of
power that reached climactic heights when
she scratched shallow rivulets and cut
deep ravines into tender flesh—
Night after endless night.
When the innocent blade made paper-thin
vents, it set free the tenacious sap that
was her life. Her heart, bereft of fresh
flow, wailed as scarlet threads flowed,
forming eddies that grew until an
inevitable power surge set free a buoyant,
carefree balloon within.
She then carved a final rune,
Kissed that last gift to herself.
Turned.
Walked away.

Julie Moulds

BONE MARROW UNIT: TRACY

I knew a man who left his wife after nine years of chemo—
left her to die, her lungs filling like someone underwater.
In my mind, she is drowning still and forever;
gasping, and making bad jokes, like the last time we talked.
She was funny, I tell my husband, *feisty funny*

with a little acid laced in. Tracy, I imagine
that other husband stating, *I want children, and a wife*
who isn't rotting, and yes, I've picked her already.
And that, I know, approaches the truth.
Whatever he said, he said it long distance,

over the phone, out east from Maine or Maryland.
He tells her he's left while she's Intensive Care,
a hygienic room in a Bone Marrow Unit in Illinois;
A week later that woman—with whom I'd laughed and walked,
other months and this, before

they siphoned the bone marrow from my blood—
a week later that woman was dead. I was asleep or drugged
and connected to six machines, but Tracy
was up that night, screaming in the tide. My husband,
wandering the halls in his yellow scrubs, paper hat,

and blue boots, had to hear, until morning, more death
than he wanted to, with me three doors away.
She was my age, thirty-two, and still
honeymooning in Florida when her cancer came.
They used to like to play tennis, she said.

Her husband had gall to fly in that last morning, looking healthy.
Had gall to make that final appearance. I tell myself
not to judge; only God can do that. Tracy had been

through more chemotherapy than anyone I ever knew—
and maybe this was the only way God could get her to die.

RENOIR'S BATHERS

What is it about women in water that almost makes them part of the landscape?
Renoir's bathers, pink and mustard and vaguely nippled; their ample thighs

rising from a purple river in a scene centered by one brown tree. What is it about women,
painted by men, that they become landscapes, creamy roses in a garden?

In another age, when people could still sleep with almost anyone, my sister and I
dipped ourselves naked in a Michigan lake, both of us, still, miraculously, virgins.

I suppose some painter in that art colony where Brenda washed dishes
could have captured us, like Renoir, two flowers with leafy thighs and brown

daisy faces. Perhaps he would accent our round hymens with petals. I want
to be the woman, with her brush, sitting in a tree above a pond where twelve

nude men are frolicking. She is painting a landscape of men: lying flat with grapes
above their open mouths; men, with buttocks turned towards her; men with arms

arched behind their long necks. She would call it *The Dozen Adonae*. Pink,
chrysanthemum men; dark, magnolia men; legs spread, organs rising or fallen,

depending on your eyes. In another time, in a deserted field, I lay naked
as a lover wrapped me in oil. I must have even walked through high grass, and,

knowing me, worried about where bugs could enter. Insects never crawl
up the legs in the paintings of the three Graces. In those landscapes

of the masculine dream, men want to paint us, perfect, from a distance.
Then break petals, like a cloud or a swan.

Wendy Bashant

LANGUOR

I am a cool Nebraskan river; my middle name is languor.
Sprawled against the prone horizon, brown and flaccid, I ooze fecundity.
Plum, Platte, Loup, Blue—flocks of cranes crowd my monosyllabic banks,
while feathers lather the shores that marry loam and silt and fertilizer.
With liquid boundaries, I am a paradox: a river without current. Still movement.
Dry driftwood sucks life from me and rots with my odorous musk.
When the morning sun strokes my body with pinks and reds,
when she rubs damp golden scents into my green flesh,
I lie still and stagnant. Silent through mud and massacres,
I lie: a cool Nebraska river, with a languorous middle name.

M. Eliza Hamilton Abégúndé

AT THE WATER SHRINE
(Loveland, Ohio)

Six hours dancing and memory comes in the slide of my foot against wood floors, in the undulation of my hips to djembe, in the chorus of moans that greet me at the shrine as I lie down to return home the only way I know.

Until now, I have only remembered the Passage. I have not had courage to remember the moment I died as the moment I lost my voice. The language of my mother and the language of my rapist converged in my throat and, unable to maneuver the simultaneous birth and death of myself, I stopped speaking.

I don't want to know what I know: the scar above my breast   the smell of burning flesh the movement of wood   my terror in the absence of trees   a man squeezing my breasts pushing my legs   the slap because I refuse again and again the beating and pushing until he believes I am nothing when in fact I have created many of me to survive.

I want to hold on to things I know are real: My mother's hand against my face   the smell of cocoa and palm oil   her fingers weaving beads in my hair   my lover's body on top of mine   market day and medicines wrapped in leaves,   drums beating out the movement of my feet my hips following the sound.

No one remembers how to place cloth under water in a wooden bowl, how to arrange flowers and stone around the altar, how to throw the coconut, how to feed the Ancestors. No one trusts the rhythm of the body to recognize home and so they follow me back and forth praying my journey from village to shrine reveals the true nature of grief.

This is where I started: at the edge of the village offering myself to the Mother of All Waters if only she would save me from this day. But I am here two centuries removed, aware I will never be saved the pain of remembering.

I am the woman watching the first merchant ship arrive, its white sails emblazoned with a red cross. I am witness to the beginning of a continent's death. I am the woman who lost her tongue to save her priesthood. I am the woman who jumped.

Memory: a woman's hand on my shoulder, someone calling my name —both inviting me back to Loveland, Ohio, a fall day, a room filled with people who will never know what it is like to enter your grave with your eyes open, listening to the waters of your birth slap good-bye against its bow.

For a long time, I do not answer. I do not want to die or be born again. I do not want to hold what I know in my heart, and I do not want to speak it. I want only to be home, a young girl, watching the horizon, dangling my legs, and enjoying for the first time the ocean washing my feet, the water so calm the sky is cloudless.

Mary Ber

GRIEF/ SUMMER

41

I have risen at dawn to birdsong,
sent life through a long, green hose to the roses,
said a sharp thing to my neighbor
and a true thing to my daughter,
thought the afternoon away on friends
as I cleaned out kitchen shelves.

Now in the dark of the moon I remember
moments of our time together
set against black leaves of loss
like sunny living photos—
sweet,
complete.

43

On my property,
in the circle of my domesticity,
under the eaves of my house
where, before we knew better,
we planted the grapevine
that doesn't belong there—
you robins settled in

I tried to poke your nest out
as I had in spring
before the vine leafed around and
tangled under.

Perched in the gutter, twigs in your beak,
you glared in anger.
From the neighbor's fence,
the dying plum tree and
rose trellises,

you launched your shrill
protest.

"OK! OK!"
I threw my pole down in disgust.
"OK, you win!"
And so I watched
you beat me to the berry bush each morning.
A tenant now,
you really had the right.

I also learned
a little of your language:
warning shrieks
each time I roamed my patio,
raw rage
if I should near the nest,
most dewy mornings and late afternoons
a cheerful chirp
assuring all was well.

Then yesterday, a different sound:
the high, demanding cries
that signal hungry children everywhere.
"Hah! Serves you right," I murmured,
wakened from the dreaming covers of my book
by shrill cacophony.

But when I went
to pick my berries,
silence hovered like
dust in the noon sun
over the flying specks
of insects
over the still and awkward bones
of the white-bellied fledgling
underneath the plum

You hadn't a thing to say,
perched in the tree
a few scant feet away.
And later still
a bush away
you went on with your harvesting
as I did mine.

But how you followed me
protesting as,
a little later on,
I bore the fledgling to the evergreens
on shovel tip,
and in a shallow hole
buried our child.

Peace, bird,
I know about death:
the moment when,
too weak to move the dirt,
you watch another
shovel it over the darling of your heart.

I know what it means
to stand outside the circle
silent and waiting
while the love of your life
star-wanders in the cosmos of his father
or sleeps
in his mother's arms.

Peace, bird,
again.
Let us sing salvation to each other.
Again, bird,
peace—
we are all out of place;
we are all at home.

Susan Firer

COMPLINE

In snow we are larger than our bodies.
    On our backs,
doing horizontal jumping
    jacks, we imprint our origin.
Looking up, we don't want
    to leave the satin-
creased skirts of snow.
    My son still thinks
it's only play this waiting until dark to go out
    & press our original body
outlines in streetlight lit pastures of snow.

He jokes: "Here is an abstract art angel."
    Then he falls
on his side, roots with his red-&-black checkered,
    earflapped hat,
and moves his legs in scissors
runs, like a dreaming dog's sleep dream chase.
I think we're all born
with this body memory. Even if no one ever taught us,
    we'd find ourselves,
as if in praise, allowing ourselves to fall
    backwards and
let our bodies' pregenetic body memory direct us.

We love snow because it is generous,
    decorative, excessive,
and motherly when we fall,
    & we do
trustingly fall back into it,
    through history,
which is time and human, through
    our mother's & father's

bodies & the bodies
of the mother & father before them.

Sometimes my son & I hold hands & fall back
together, like skyjumpers.
Other times we watch the critical
beauty of each others'
effort set again toward only beauty
toward looking up & accepting
the lake winds & pelting
snow. We leave our bodies'
gratitude in snow.

Jude Rittenhouse

SNAKE HANDS

The Serpent Goddess...like the great rivers of the earth winding from mountain to sea, traces the spiraling life energy...represents...the primordial waters encircling the earth.

The Myth of the Goddess
By Anne Baring and Jules Cashford

Blue snakes bulge beneath this skin
like my mother's, like my grandmothers':
a woman's hands. Though mine do not
bake or crochet or raise children
endless as fields of wheat on the prairie.

My hands do not have
the force of my father's mother:
Mom's apple pies, sweet as Summer winds
yet tart as that season's sharp ending;
her deceptively simple yet rich chocolate
cake baked while whipping boarding house
and six children into shape alone—husband off
working for the railroad.

My hands will not find
the secret measure of my mother's mother:
Nana's fried fritters drenched in oil and sugars
enchanting grandchildren to assist and listen
to her nap-time stories of Missouri fishermen
finding wild bears and honey—told while her husband
sulked in his bedroom, vexed that she alone
could charm all these children.

My hands will never smooth
the clammy forehead of a child; these fingers
cannot weave that mythic promise of safety

like my Mother's hands tried and tried.
Nor will they dig, weed, plant seeds, and clip only
to see Nature sneak it all back to her own
vision of beauty and there will be no grandchildren
needing knitted blankets—while a husband
sits waiting, impatient for attention.

These hands felt blue rivers, fish-filled
with possibility, slipping through fingers
held careful, wide open, willfully releasing
old spells to make a bargain—to cling
for survival to this pen like a life-raft,
to pour out these rivers, these bulging blue snakes,
to flow toward that place where woman-blood
encircles this world and weeps self-contained.

ELLA'S DAKOTA QUILT

Ella finished mowing the day's last hay,
drove toward home where he'd be waiting:
hungry for her, waiting for supper.

The heavy tractor bumped
past her proud corn near ready and sunflower heads
drooped heavy, weighted with Summer's warmth,
past her patient stripes of wheat: green planted late
next to gold ripe to cut beside bronze
where crop lay drying
bordered by black fresh-turned soil
waiting to grow again.

She thought about the sun looking down on Dakota,
about the quilt of land, sewn with her sweat,
for the Lord to see, pronounce good.

The roaring tractor thrummed and bounced.
Ella gripped tight, saw cracked hands steer:

hands that never reached beyond baking, canning,
cooking, quilting, caring,
until that day ten years ago
(when she still hoped for children growing),
that day he turned too hard, too fast,
lay crushed in his field beneath metal's weight
until after sunset, she went looking,
found her fate.

The poplars she had planted to protect that field
must look like tatting, like lace, to the Lord;
her corn's silk tasseled tops like cross-stitch,
her fresh-rolled hay rows
like some mythic monster's droppings:
some beast whose footprints, filled with rain,
became sparkling sequins for the Lord and sun above.

The tractor shuddered to stillness.
She dismounted, still vibrating deeply
to her bones
filled by prairie's evening chorus
roaring toward forever.

She felt him willing her to him,
wanting supper, craving her
company after eternal day alone.

Ella dallied on the porch,
surveyed the wide lands she'd raised up, cut back
and sometimes lost—like the children she'd never had.
She watched the west go colors
to make her heart ache, her soul shiver,
and she knew the Lord was no bearded old man
but something inside her
looking out through her eyes.

Sandra Sidman Larson

NATIVE THOUGHTS

My bones are laced together now with Ojibwa soil.
I hear the cracking of lost hopes

tall grasses, the last breath of the prairie,
language thrown into open graves.

Many circle with wheels of blame.
The People try to explain

in smoke, in drink, the weariness
of moving on. I came here thirty years ago

escaping other ancestors into a land where
ancestors are not allowed but remain.

I lived beside them in the pine period of life, the resin
of muscles drying on red pines with bloody backs.

I have hung my children permanently on their father's
family tree where snowflakes wheel in cold air.

The old Indian staggered toward me and told me no
white community organizers were welcome in his circle.

White pines waited. So I'm told I can only have my own
ancestors, but they are not listening, buried on the coast.

In the gym we expect the fancy dancers next,
the sweet percussion of silver bells jingling.

My world discounts the drumming of each heart.
Grandmothers here learn words for gone

***

wrap hopes in blankets
and dress for the occasion.

The laden tables of these broken fields
offer a blessing and I rise like smoke to grasp it.

This granite ground is stony nourishment
with hopes drifting toward the horizon.

Walking toward the footsteps of my poems
one thousand miles from loss, the Rockies rise.

They are to the west of my intentions.
I am here whether any one wants me or not.

ECTOPIC PREGNANCY, NORTHWESTERN UNIVERSITY

for Loopy

Last night I was on all fours like a cat, creeping
down the hall toward the dorm mother's room,
a small shaft of light under the door.

Nestled in a tube instead of the riverbed of me,
I could not pour you a form or a future.
The surgeon said you'd lost your way.

Standing at the edge of the roar-vast lake,
I listen as the waves thump to the shore.
You are gone. This day, only half-eaten,
I find my way back past the North Shore Hotel,

catch sight of a ladies' luncheon scattered
in coffee cups, pools of ice cream melted by
the warmth of painted chatter. I am distracted by

the hammering of a construction drill

and my own silence. I turn toward school,
knowing I am moving away from a distance
that cannot be traveled.

TO NAME THE COLOR GREEN IS A SOURCE OF FLIGHT

Here the earth is rusted by November
all the moist greenery grown dry
tree hands make their final
fragile wave & prairies dance
with abandon in the billowy winds.
The landscape open now, no pretenses
just a hand-me-down wardrobe for earth.

Soon a parade of crystals weave
a quilt of white over the russet & red
ground & obscure the earth's golden hair.

A poem has a mission something like fall—
to be open, to hear the wind
to let moist mystery die slowly
to let the whiteness of words cover
what falls, to leave time for hope—
the coming of the first leaf shadows of spring.

Terry Lee Schifferns

DEAR BOBBIE

Dear Bobbie,

It's been a vintage year
for wind and storms.
First, the heat—90's
and that damn unforgiving wind.
Got the garden in late
the landlord sprayed—
killed the tomatoes and peppers
but I suppose I'll try again,
though it's awfully late in the season.

And the storms—
Afternoons, the thunderheads
move in from the southwest,
the sky dips low
until there is no margin
between cloud and ground.

We study the horizon
for the promised pirouette of destruction;
feeling cheated somehow
when it fails to avail
for us the story
we had already begun
when we repaired to the cellar
with candle in hand
but not going down
daring, instead, to stand outside
and watch the blue jeans
on the line
flap frantic
in their out-of-body dance.

In the morning I find a nest
on the ground
and a swallow chatters
from the tree above.
I think of you,
far away, in Arizona,
Your new home.
It's been a good summer
but, I miss you.
Terry lee

(2)

Bobbie,
Night storms regularly—
Lightning springs intermittent,
the sparked release of humidity trapped in heat,
across the darkened sky.

Plenty of rain,
so much,
the nest I found
and set on the ledge outside
has begun to sprout
secret shoots of pale grass.

As an act of faith
I replanted
tomatoes and peppers.
The soil,
after three years of thick mulch
looks so rich and loamy
yet,
lurking within its sterile secret molecules
is the plant cancer
probably Atrazine
that wilts and kills

all except the weeds,
that have grown immune to its threat.
I water relentlessly
believing.

In the late afternoon,
I release my thoughts
like pollen
to be carried across the miles
to Arizona, your new home.

When you catch whispers
of sweet sage scent
and fresh mown hay
that do not belong
in the dry desert breeze,
you'll know they come from me.

Send me desert secrets.
Terry lee

(3)

Dear Bobbie,

Waiting for the sun to warm,
sunbound pepper, tomato, and parsley plants grow
leggy on the kitchen windowsill.
The need to plant and grow
fevered in an early February thaw.

Today, lilac scent
sends me prowling
the Platte's south bank
in search
of spring's promised

feast, morels.

I gather them in hushed thanks.

And then,
beneath cottonwoods just leafing
tender green, a robin egg
blue enough to flutter
any imagination, calls out to me.
I carry it home to nest
among Gila River rocks, runes
from another place and day,
saguaro spine and whitened turtle bones
on the mantle; altar
for believers
in the oracle whisper
within all things.

Tonight in the cactus forest
where you are now,
cup the prairie to your ear
and listen hard.
It's me.

Terry lee

Chicago Bridal Portrait: The Best Man's A Cat
photograph by
Scotty Denhollem, 1982.

Prose

Marilyn Krysl

DIRT

Dirt. As a kid I liked its soft, powdery feel between my toes, and the way you could dust things with it—earth's talcum. Summer days I wandered my grandparents' wheat farm, tossing up small tornadoes of dust in the corral, sitting and sifting this fine stuff through my fingers. Stunned by heat those long afternoons, I stirred water into a pan of dirt. Magical, this mixing of two elements. So unlike each other, dirt and water, they became together a third thing, new creation. Stirring suggested food, and the combine's flat lengths of tin looked like cookie sheets. I laid out my delectables and left them, baking.

Dirt and water: this was the primal goo, the basic material of the universe. One day I mixed up a pan of mud and made an Adam and Eve. Arms, legs, hair. She had breasts, he had a penis. I remembered though that they were innocent, they couldn't see each other's nakedness. So I gave them no eyes. Their mouths cried out in the wilderness of dark. I mixed up a pan of brownies.

I fed my creations, and while they ate I began the long contemplation. The Bible said dirt was what people were made of. *From dust thou comest, to dust thou shalt return.* Everybody came originally from dirt, I thought. Everything came from it. Dirt was everywhere, it was what the earth itself was made of. It made sense that everything came from this substance. Dirt was precious stuff, our basic material. Elemental, magical. Dirt was not dirty, it was a sacred powder. I began to construct a philosophy of dirt.

Dirt was sacred stuff, the earth was sacred ground. Holy. I piled dirt in a cracked blue willow bowl, set it on top of a box, lit a candle beside it. I knelt before this altar, murmured devotional incantations. The air agreed with my procedures. Water running underground seconded my motions. I had made a shrine, I held services. At the close I stood and sang *America The Beautiful.*

Digging graves was all right. It was right to bury the dead, it was fitting to put them back where they'd come from. I understood that leaves and dead people decayed, these things returned to the elements. When my Adam and Eve began to crumble, I scooped out a hole and laid them in, covered them. I stood over this funeral a long time with the hose, watering. I thought how Adam and Eve were losing themselves, becoming ground.

Gardening too seemed a permissible way to work the earth. Fat worms drilled their passageways through topsoil, giving the roots of plants an airing. Loosening the top of the ground with a spade seemed to let the earth breathe. When I turned earth over with a trowel and crumbled it in my fingers, it fluffed up. You could tell dirt liked being handled. Handling would feel to the earth the way it felt to me, like the good roughness of my grandmother's hand rubbing my back.

I had doubts about tractors though. They made a terrible noise and their blades sliced. These brutally clean cuts weren't the same as my digging. I thought this was an important distinction. It seemed important because I thought the ground could feel what we did to it. Dirt felt my hands in it. It liked being handled, as I liked being hugged and held. On hot days it liked my mixing it with cool water. I talked to dirt, told it stories and sang it songs, stories and songs, those things I liked so well myself. *Do unto others as you would have them do unto you.* I tried not to hurt beetles, I was good to grass. It seemed self-evident that we owed the ground every consideration.

I was not in favor of building dams, and I didn't approve of oil well drilling either. The dynamiting of perfectly good hillsides upset me. I didn't think men driving bulldozers should smash down fine stands of wild grass and weeds, leaving behind the imprint of tire treads. "Why are they doing that?" I asked my grandmother. "They're just building a road," she'd say. Did we need another road? How many roads did it take to get from one place to another? One, I thought, was plenty.

Stories of the Gold Rush made the miners sound like men gone mad with greed. But even before I heard those stories I felt uneasy about mining. I didn't like to imagine picks hacking away at a mountainside. Hacking rock seemed brutal. It hurt the mountainside. The rock could feel it. Rock was sentient, not quite in the same way animals and plants were sentient, but in its own way, rock's way.

I felt in the features of the landscape a resonance. Earth's electromagnetic web? I felt vibration. I was a sounding body for the Schumann resonance. I stood amidst the trilling presence of my surroundings. I stood amidst a field, like the field around a magnet. I was alive amidst myriad live presences. I registered the sentience of lakes, hillsides. And I worried. We were hurting things, I thought. I worried about the sensitivity of leaf, hollow and stone.

My grandparents had a mulberry tree and on good days I climbed this tree and looked out across distance. I swayed on my branch like a girl at the top of a mast, and I thought I could see the curvature of the earth. I could feel it, way out there, starting to curve down. Anything that big had its own plan, I thought. It wouldn't do to try to move things around on the globe as if they were furniture. Let things just lie there the way they are, I thought. If the earth wanted to move things, it could make an earthquake or a volcano or a flood. If the earth made a cave of the winds or cut out a channel for a river, it knew what it was doing. Those things were earth's business, I thought. Let earth do those things. Who were we to interfere?

There was nothing to do with these feelings of mine. No one I knew shared them. Eventually l learned not to voice them. I worked to tear myself from these feelings, I tore myself away and was torn. But at the time, in my solitary moments, I registered earth's irritation and wondered. When no one was watching I held a rock to my ear and listened, calling the universe for news. And sometimes I knelt and laid my ear against the ground. I heard, far down, a grumbling, like thunder in the distance, but round, a spherical grumbling, vast in its dimensions, a sound as large as earth itself. It was, I thought, the moan of a creatureous thing, the audible irritation of a great being. I'd been right, I thought. We shouldn't be bothering dirt with bulldozer and dynamite. Like anyone, the earth needed soothing. We ought to be patting and smoothing, watering and blanketing. We ought to be talking to and singing to and reassuring our ground.

I did not know, as a child, the true extent to which the earth had reason for irritation. I mixed dirt and water and did not know about the Trinity test, about Hiroshima and Nagasaki, about testing of the hydrogen bomb in the Marshall islands. I did not know of these events, but I heard and took note of the earth's muttering. Now I think what I had then was a wonderfully irrational wisdom. Ancient people felt metals had a life of their own, like animals. Stone was the concentrated power of earth. Precious stones were frozen nectar, the life force crystallized. Thales, a Greek physicist, believed chunks of amber were alive. Native Americans know mountains are living beings, wind caves are the mountains' lungs. They breathe; this breath can be recorded. We have measured the breath of caves at the base of the San Francisco peaks in Arizona. They inhale and exhale at 30 mph in six-hour cycles. Smoholla the Dreamer said, "The white man tells me *plow the ground.* Shall I take a knife and tear my mother's breast? The-white man tells me *quarry stone.* Shall I dig beneath her skin for bones?" Claude Kuwanijuma, a Hopi, said, "The stones remember. If you know how to listen they will tell you many things."

In my lifetime physicists have been among those listening. Physicists have been listening to rocks, and what they hear is what Claude Kuwanijuma heard. Listening to parts, they hear the whole. They hear the whole, David Bohm's *that-which-is.* Physics has noticed that the basic bits of the universe are not truly particulate. What is going on in and around us is not the still presence of chunks of inanimate matter, but a process. As Gary Zukhov writes in *The Dancing Wu Li Masters*, the basic "unit" of the universe is an event. And events in one place mesh with all the other events in all the other places. As John Archibald Wheeler declared at the 1981 Nobel Conference, this universe is a participatory universe. And we are in it, alive amidst liveness. We're alive, and here we go, here we have been going. What there is is that whole, *that-which-is.* Whether we like it or not, we are of the whole. We are bound into each other and into the world. This universe is a matrix of sentience.

Playing rock telephone, it seems, wasn't so silly after all. My notion that dirt liked watering on hot days was a notion wiser than I knew. I lacked knowledge, but I had wisdom. I was paying attention or, as Buddhism teaches, being mindful, not with a child's arbitrary fantasy, but in an important, vital way. I was paying attention to what went on in me and around me. The elements were like me—I was of them. The elements and I were made from the same stuff. Waterfall and volcano, parrot and pickerel were like me, I was like them. And I could deduce from the way I felt how fine dirt felt getting sprinkled, how well grass liked being left alone to flourish. How birds fluffed up with well-being when they were sung to, how crickets and beetles profited from storytelling. And how the trunk and branches of the mulberry tree appreciated bodily contact as much as I did. How light needed our prayerful attention. How darkness rested in our sleep.

Our lives depend on such attending. Not attending can hurt us. What we know now is how little we know, we who prided ourselves on being realistic. We held up reality as an absolute, the final arbiter. We imagined we knew, pretty much, what reality was. Now we know that our ignorance is vast and dangerous. We don't know where and when to touch or not to touch. "Look—see that flame? The stove is hot." We know about as much as the child who hears his mother say this for the first time.

Knowing we are ignorant may be useful. There is knowledge and there is wisdom. We are ignorant but we may still be wise. Ignorant, we become cautious. Ignorance transforms us into watchers, listeners. We sift dirt through our fingers, feel its texture, become attentive. What will constitute wise attendance?

There is doing and there is being. Wise attendance is wise being. It is more than disinterested observation, as we are more than recorders, collectors of data. We are part of the data. We are sentient creatures, of the mesh, of the whole, that-which-is. In a very special, important way we are what we attend. When we hurt what only seems to be outside us, we hurt ourselves. In the most vital way imaginable, we are not disinterested but interested.

Sentient beings, we wander the earth, drink the water, eat the fruit, sit on the ground. Knowledge of our ignorance brings us down to ground level. Ground level is human level, sentient level. There are no microscopes at ground level, human level. There are no instruments. Sitting in the dirt, without instruments, we are sentient creatures. Sitting in the dirt, without instruments, we begin to see.

We see mite and sprout, feel heat and light. We hear wind and water. We pick up handfuls of dirt, we begin to wonder. Sentient, we notice we're here, in and of the universe. From this perspective, everything is as important as everything else. Sitting in the dirt, we are at last in a position to become philosophers. Finally we understand deforestation hurts the forest, the granite upthrust registers the blast.

I would mix again some dirt, some water. I would fashion another Eve, another Adam. I would give them genitals again, those necessary parts. But this time I would also give them eyes. Let them sit on the ground and gaze at each other. They compare, they notice the differences between them. And they notice as well the similarities. Both have hair, both have legs, arms, fingers, faces. A nose, a mouth. Ears. And those eyes.

When they have looked their fill at each other they notice where they are. They notice the earth beneath them. Eve picks up a handful of dirt, feels it. Adam picks up a rock, puts it to his ear. Eve's fingers register the texture of dirt, its fineness. In sunlight the dirt looks bright. Suddenly, a sound. *Was* that a sound, over there where the leaves moved? Eve pokes Adam. He takes the rock from his ear, looks where she's pointing. Leaves. A bird?

Sunlight, a breeze, insects, flowering shrubs, grasses. These things are a felt field. There is something in the air, an animation, an expectancy. The clearing where they sit has a life of its own, their own.

They look around, they listen. Now Adam too picks up a handful of dirt. There's something here, he thinks, something it seems important to notice. He pours his handful of dirt into Eve's hand. They examine this dirt, they notice in it some quickening energy. Isn't it bright, this dirt, and alive inside its texture. They feel the life stuff sparking in it as they sift it through their fingers. They begin to notice they are not alone.

Barbara Esstman

WHAT THE RIVERS TEACH US

People often ask where I get the ideas for my books, and I say they come gradually and piece-meal from everything I've ever learned; they are discovered as I write, and combined in ways I never would have expected. Sometimes at first even I don't recognize the specific source. The first image of what would become *Night Ride Home* was of a woman very alone in the center of Missouri farmland, with something of death around her. I didn't know her, nor why she was paralyzed by grieving. I wouldn't suspect for two years that she might fall in love. But I did recognize the place: St. Charles, the small town outside of St. Louis where I grew up.

My father owned the St. Charles grain elevator, and we often visited the farms belonging to his customers and friends. I remember climbing on combines like jungle gyms and watching black Angus graze like overgrown pets; I caught my first fish when I was five, sitting on the banks of the Cuivre River, which ran along the boundary of a dairy farm dappled with black and white Holsteins.

My family loved to drive the country roads that radiated out from town. Before air conditioning was a given, we went for rides in the evening to escape from our house, heated up to sauna-like levels during the day, and the air blowing in the car windows cooled us. As we passed the many fields, my father taught my brother and me how to identify the grains by the differences in the beards of each variety, and he named them for us like a litany: wheat, oats, rye, barley, milo. Later, as a teenager, I cruised those same roads with my friends, far from our parents, and I parked on the more deserted ones with my boyfriend in his old black Plymouth.

So I knew immediately the place of that first image: the town of St. Charles, transformed into the place of the novel, LaCote—built on low hills along the Missouri River and surrounded by farmland, much of which was on flood plain.

My family lived in town, on high ground that was never in danger, but my father's grain elevator was near the steep river bank behind Main Street. One of my earliest and most powerful memories is standing with him there when I was six, during a summer when the rivers had flooded the Midwest. His elevator was a huge, old place with catwalks above the deep bins, mousers nursing their kittens on feed sacks, and an adding machine in the office that I was allowed to play with. Usually when he took me along with him we walked down to look at the river before going home. Usually it flowed past a ten-foot incline and we looked out across to the bottoms land on the other side and the flat fields there.

But on that particular day in the summer of 1953, the river was so high that it overran the steep bank, covering the KATY tracks that ran parallel to it and the alley that ran parallel to them, all the way into the shed next to the elevator. Instead of feed sacks stacked inside, sand bags formed a low wall, and the expanse of ground stretching out from the far bank had disappeared entirely, turned by the flood into one vast sea.

So the place of the novel brought with it a time of flood, and eventually the flood of the novel was made from my memories of all the Missouri floods I had seen or heard about: of water moccasins being left behind by receding waters; traffic horses blocking submerged roads; lines of sandbags built into war bunkers; and farm land covered to the horizon with what seemed like a great lake.

Most specifically, the flood of the novel came from 1993, when the book was in its early stages and I came home a few weeks after the rivers had crested. My mother's friend, Helen, whom I'd grown up with and always visited when back in St. Charles, took me for a drive out around Portage des Sioux where her son and daughter-in-law owned a farm. Enough of the flood was left that I got a taste of what it had been like at full force. I stood on her son's back porch, six or seven miles from the river's usual banks, and looked out over what had been fields. The river spread over all I could see, and waves lapped up to the bottom of the rise his house stood safe on.

Then Helen drove me out to where the waters had gone down, to places no one remembered ever having been flooded before. I saw the abandoned home of another friend, the windows and doors blown out by the river rushing through and what was left of the structure looking dirty and sad as if it had been deserted years before. We drove through land where the corn was stunted or rotted, where trees stood dying from having their roots submerged and where every structure put there by humans was punched, crushed, or twisted, that is, those that hadn't been washed away.

We talked about what came next. Who had given up and moved to higher ground. Who had started to clean up and resume their old lives. How the silt brought by the flood had enriched the ground, but how the farmers would have to work to get rid of the weeds that had come with that silt to previously clear fields. How those whose lives were disrupted found ways to adjust and how strangers and friends had formed a community of mutual help.

When I returned to my home in Virginia, I brought back this new flood to add to my draft of *Night Ride Home*. Each novel must have a world with dimension and detail for the characters to move in, but geographical place also becomes psychic landscape. In other words, the location, with its particular beauties and hazards, is not only meant as literal ground for the characters to stand on but as their metaphoric and psychological state.

Rivers and floods, whether real or imagined, shape those people or characters who live with them. While some humans are arrogant enough to believe they can control whatever they put their minds to, floods give a lesson in humility and respect for forces greater than our own. Nothing to do but acknowledge the water's strength and accept that heroic efforts might at best save a small area from damage.

Floods show us that we must depend on our families, neighbors, or people we didn't especially like or know or will ever see again, to help us build dikes or reinforce levees or give us shelter or food or comfort. Or maybe to just stand with us overlooking the water and say "damn" softly under their breaths.

Rivers teach us the rhythms of nature that we often ignore. We forget—or maybe just don't want to think about—the cycles of rise and fall, bounty and loss, stillness and action. Unlike the quick strikes of a fire or an earthquake, floods settle in like meditations, force us to study their effects, and make us wait before they give back the land for us to reclaim.

Then when the land begins to reappear, we see it piece by piece, the way we do the parts of an answer to a problem we are working out. Or the scenes of a novel being written. The way Nora, the woman in

Night Ride Home, has to try to rebuild her life bit by bit after the death of her son, a death she can no more stop than the Missouri River that floods her land.

Ridgely Jackson

SCRIMMAGE

It's 10:30 p.m., and I've just gotten home from my first writing class. Even as my key slides into the dead bolt, I know my son's got the volume turned up too high. The bass vibrates the landing outside our apartment.

When I open the door, the entryway swells with a graveled female voice roaring the blues. "Summer time-time-time, child. The living's easy." I smile. Janis and Big Brother. Matthew has raided my stash of sixties music. He doesn't realize yet that he has the same taste in music as his mother.

I walk down the narrow hallway to his room and stand in the doorway. "I'm home." Matthew doesn't hear me over the music, so I go into his bedroom and turn down the volume. "I'm home," I say again and sit on the bed. I look first at Matthew, who mumbles but doesn't look up from his homework, and then at the dark TV screen. "Any Diana news?" I ask. Diana, Princess of Wales, has been dead for four days. She died at 36. Janis Joplin died at 27. The Queen of Hearts and the Queen of Rock.

My son, who often ignores me until he forgets himself, finally looks up from his homework. He tries to suppress a grin, and I know he thinks he's about to say something clever. "They said Diana's still dead, Ma. And that you should get a life."

I smile. "I'm trying, kid. I'm trying. That's why I'm taking this class."

"So how'd it go?" He's being uncommonly conversant.

"Terrible. Discouraging. I'm in over my head."

"You always say that."

"It's true. Our first story is due next week, and the teacher never told us how to write one. I haven't a clue. Honey, do you think we could catch something about Diana on CNN?"

"No, Ma. You're addicted to Diana."

"I'm not. Hardly at all." Matthew makes no move to produce the remote needed to turn on the television, so I continue. "Ya know, there are people in my class with college degrees. They're published.

Screenwriters. A doctor even. People who make their living writing."

"Scrimmaging with the varsity, hey?"

I picture Matthew limping to the car after football practice, always ready to display his bruises and scratches and swollen joints. He plays football the same way Janis belts out a song. With abandon. I ask him, "The sophomores scrimmage with the varsity? Is that safe?"

"Of course it's not safe, mother," he declares proudly. "Where will safe get you?"

I hope this is fifteen-year old bravado talking and not the fifteen-year-old's football coach. I try to ask casually, "Is that what your coach tells you?"

"He says to let go when you scrimmage the varsity. Be wild. Go for it." He looks me straight in the eye. "Play as if you've got nothing to lose. Because you don't." Matthew spews forth his adolescent wisdom and returns to his homework.

I stare at the blank TV screen as my mind goes back over the writing class. Maybe I missed something. Maybe the teacher did give us a clue. He read us a story. It seemed like a Jack Kerouac kind of thing, but instead of going on and on about a road, the writer went on and on about a tree stump. Maybe I could write about my lifetime as a clerical worker. That would be at least as exciting as a tree stump.

I interrupt my son's studying and try to reignite the conversation. "What else did your coach tell you?"

"Ma," he protests, "I'm trying to finish this."

"Just tell me, or I'll turn on—"

"Okay, okay. He told us to play hardest at the end of the game even though you're tired, and that hard work pays off. Oh, and he said that the pain goes away when you win."

Matthew's gaze lowers to his books. "That's all I remember."

I stare at the dark TV screen some more. It occurs to me that staring at the TV while it's off is not all that different from staring at it while it's on. My mind returns to the writing class.

The teacher had said,"Turn personal experiences into fiction." My personal experiences as a typist aren't too compelling. On the other hand, I did make it to San Francisco for the sixties. When my friends left home for Marquette and U of I, I left home for Haight and Ashbury. I got there a couple years after Janis and acid rock arrived. I stayed long after Janis died and Starbucks had come to the Haight. Unfortunately, I didn't realize I was experiencing history. If I'd known then about this writing class, I would have paid closer attention.

Images channel surf through my mind. The Fillmore. The Trident. Wavy Gravy. Ken Kesey's psychedelic bus. They used to park the Merry Prankster's bus outside Cody's Bookstore on Telegraph and obstruct the view of the Bubble Lady who spent her days balancing on stilts and blowing soap bubbles at the hippies who walked by. A banner on the rear of the bus announced its destination: "Further."

Back in those days, it never occurred to me that I wasn't going there, too. Janis reigned, and I was in motion. But by the time of Diana's rule, I had stopped. It was easier to watch someone else move.

"Ma, here — take it."

I look up from the blank set. My son extends his hand and offers me the remote. "Ten minutes of Diana. That's all you get."

"Maybe I'll pass."

"Way to go, Ma. You can do it."

"You think so?"

"Yeah. Cold turkey."

I stand up and kiss him good night. "Your parental unit is leaving now."

"They don't say that anymore. That was about two years ago."

"I'm slow."

"I know."

I move towards the door.

"Ma, I just thought of something else the coach told us. You still want to know?"

"Sure."

"Play from the heart. When you scrimmage, you've got to play from the heart. Like me."

"Like you."

"Goodnight, Ma."

Before I leave the room, I turn the volume back up so we can hear Janis sing.

Deborah Shouse

COUNTER CULTURE

Minnesota

My partner and I are on a journey. We travel long in the car and by the end of the day, I am hungry for something. I want the sizzle and smell of food; I want to see the poetry of preparation, to feel the heat, hassle and hustle of kitchen. I want to walk into a strange place and strike up small talk that might grow large. I want to be a part of the counter culture.

"What's good today?"

"Pass that sugar, will you?"

"You done with the sports section?"

"Which is better, the pecan or cherry pie?"

We sit at a Minnesota counter, miles from familiar territory, and we are at home.

Wisconsin

There is no hostess, just a man in bib overalls at a center stool and a bored cook lounging against the grill.

The cook butts out his cigarette and listens to our order. He flattens the gangly curl of bacon, scoops spatula under eggs, presses lid over the tops of hash browns, slashes butter across the tanned cheeks of toast, tosses jam packets onto waiting plates, and suddenly three of us, the man in overalls, the writer, and her partner, are fed.

Illinois

We're driving late, and our car coughs and sputters. We crawl it into a gas station and wait for the tow truck at the only lit-up spot in town, the Back Alley Cafe.

Even though it is almost closing time, Boon gives us a spot at the counter.

"Sit as long as you want," he invites. "We still have to clean up."

Boon bought the cafe after he got laid off from the Ford plant for the third time. Plus, he and his wife, they wanted their own business.

"Fixing good food is a lot of work," Boon says, as he hands us fries, grilled cheese sandwiches and cherry colas.

Tonight, he works the counter, while the high school track star and the cheerleader wait on tables, bus and do the dishes.

"Have you got my pizza?" A young woman rushes in, a baby slung over one shoulder, a diaper bag over the other.

"Right here," Boon says.

"We're the only ones in town who make pizza," he explains to us. "You have to give the people what they want."

He gives us what we want: shelter, conversation and good food.

Iowa

She bursts from her black tight jeans and white tee shirt. She chomps gum while she pours the coffee and tells the harried cook our order. Then she stares out the window of the cafe, while two more out-of-towners sit at the counter.

"I wish the movie stars would come back," she says, rousing herself, automatically getting two glasses of water, cocoons of silverware.

Clint Eastwood and Meryl Streep, they were here, filming, she says.

"Clint sat there." She points to the stool on my left. "He ordered cherry pie and coffee."

Her eyes glaze over.

"My boyfriend picked him up from the airport, so of course he drove him here. Clint gave me a big tip. I wish he'd come back."

She wanders into the back room and our order appears on the ledge that separates the kitchen from the world. We see our eggs, shimmering with delicate frothiness, and our hearty hashbrowns. Our breakfast, so close and yet not within reach. Our waitress, back in the back reapplying her lipstick, and our food gathering the cold air. I put my hand on the stool next to me and wish she'd come back.

Nebraska

The ticket snapped into the metal holder means Lorraine flows into action. It's lovemaking with the same old man—she doesn't even need to look to crack the eggs and whisk them into obedience, slap buns on the grill, tame the flat pink promise of hamburger with a metal sheath so pattie will submit to bun.

Lorraine is competent and dour, until Evan, the man next to me, says her name.

I watch as her face floats into a smile, the wrinkles abandoned in a Technicolor web of Mary Kaye.

"Ain't seen you around much," she murmurs. She leans against the counter, her body a flirtation device.

"Yeah," Evan says, his face blank.

"'I've been brushing up my bowling game," Lorraine says to Evan. "I like to try new stuff, you know. I like to try...anything."

She tosses hints, hoops and hollers. But he doesn't order anything from her grill, just listens, then moves to talk to another guy about the wreck on the highway.

Lorraine looks at me and at my partner, who is reading the local paper. For a moment, Lorraine and I know each other too well. Then she flips the bacon, presses the hamburger, slides toast down, slices a tomato, everything slow and orchestrated. She doesn't hurry; she knows the ending: a plate with toast, eggs and bacon. Only the heart is not cooked just right.

Missouri

Beside me a frazzle-haired woman with a raspy voice cuts her cornbread into little pieces and slathers each with butter.

"I just got back from court and my nerves are shot," she says.

Our elbows brush and I say, "Why were you in court?"

Her story is long and winding, moving through a bowl of beans, two pieces of cornbread and a towering meringue of lemon pie.

Her story settles inside me, filling as whipped potatoes.

"You'll be old someday," she tells me. "And you'll be grateful when someone listens to you."

Kansas

Once home, we sink into our regular restaurants—the pink linen tablecloths, the creamy crockery plates, not cracked or stained by too much use, the plush isolation of the corner booth.

We order Pesce Venetizia and Pasta Primavera. The food is more varied, more exotic, more healthful than diner fare. The atmosphere is more restful.

I eat my succulent food, wipe my mouth with the linen napkin, and yearn for the counter culture.

Laura Distelheim

ON NINA, NIGHTINGALES AND SURVIVING THE NIGHT

I know as soon as I open the door that Chicago has emerged from the tunnel of winter. The air has lost its sting, the sky its charcoal veil. By the time we arrive at the park, the jungle gym is blooming with children. A pigeon swoops low across our path and Nina leans forward in her stroller, arms outstretched. "Hiya!" she calls, and when I laugh, she laughs, too, as though she knows: The soft breeze that ruffles her curls is scented with victory for me, is redolent with the fragrance of a springtime earned, not given.

I lift her into my arms and carry her across the grass, thinking of days when neither would have been possible. "Hokay!" she says, her breath warm against my ear, and I pause—feel the hug of chubby legs around my waist, the pat pat pat of tiny fingers on my neck, the feathery brush of silken skin against my cheek—before slipping her into the swing. I push, she claps, the sunlight deepens, the moment sings.

She's not my baby. She's my niece, but more—a sistergift, who came into this world at a time when it had gone dark for me. At a time when a disease of many syllables and even more symptoms had toppled the life I had been building. Had stolen my energy first, my immunity soon after. Had inflamed my joints, my nodes, my muscles, my skin. Had sent me surfing through month after month after month on waves of chills and sweats and nausea. Had eventually settled into a lingering weakness that made me battle for every step, until I could no longer move freely, youngly, across this earth. Until, pressing forward into darkness, I began to disbelieve the possibility of light.

Nina was fifteen minutes into her life when I first held her in my arms, a five pound, four ounce sliver of the future swaddled in pale pink flannel. I looked down to see my sister's eyes looking back from a rosebud face, and knew that the universe had just been reinvented. That winter, Nina and I sat often by the window, two slow people in a fast-moving world, watching the snow bathe the city in pearly light. Propped upon my lap, her fuzzy head against my heart, she listened while I spun tales of the life before her. And when I became too tired to talk, we listened to the silence together: A car horn bleating in the distance. The elevator doors clicking shut. A child calling, a dog barking, on the sidewalk eight stories below. An aria leaking through the ceiling from a stereo somewhere above. The soft pant pant of her breathing, as she sat propped against my heart.

Over a period throughout the spring, both my career and a new relationship succumbed to my illness, descending like two kites that had lost the wind, taking independence, identity and belonging along with them. It was in that springtime, too, that Nina first became my groupie. "AAAAAAAHHH!" she would squeal, clapping and rocking, whenever I walked into a room, even if I had walked out but a moment before. "AAAAAAAAHHH!" I would remind myself, later, in the night, when the ache of loss throbs with most insistence.

I was stalked through that summer by the haunting awareness that illness had made me less than I'd once been. It was a reality that greeted me anew every morning, tracked me through each day, crept behind me, taunting, into sleep. It was with me one afternoon when I went into Nina's nursery, where she'd awakened, startled, from her nap. When I reached to gather her to me, she buried her face in my shoulder and clung, never doubting that I could slay the monster who'd just chased her through her dreams. She clung and I sang and we rocked—until her sobs had quieted and slowed, until the light slanted silver through the window and the monster lay heaped on the floor, until I knew that, at least for that moment, I was everything I needed to be.

"Pfffft," Nina said to me one day in early autumn, and then waited, to see if I would laugh. I laughed. It soon seemed her mission: to make me laugh. "Pfffft," she would begin, and then open and close her mouth, put her finger in her nose, puff her cheeks, vibrate her lips, flutter her lashes against my face. And when I laughed, she laughed, too, even longer, looking at me through my sister's eyes, begging me not to stop.

When winter arrived, Nina thought about walking, but decided against it. It was my turn to cheer her on. We formed a squad, her parents, grandparents, and I, marched around her, applauded her, chanted, "Walking, walking, walking, walking," while she sat on the floor, smiling up at us and wriggling her toes. Eventually, she clutched our hands and shuffled, pausing to applaud herself every now and then. Even more eventually, she gripped the table and slid, more gripping than sliding, though, so we clapped and we chanted and we waited. And then, suddenly, it all happened at once, not long before springtime returned: Remission, my doctor called it. ("Walk to Aunt Laura," her daddy said.) But to me, it seemed a reawakening. (And she goose-stepped into my arms.)

When I look at Nina now, I sometimes see the girl of ten, the woman of twenty she will become. When I someday look at the woman, I will see the baby still. The baby who is the reason I have come to this springtime knowing that the possibility of light survives the shadows; that this randomly careening world produces tenors as well as terrorists; that even while the staccato shriek of gunfire stabs Sarajevo's dusk, there is Paris, where the golden lullaby of church bells serenades the melting sun. I will see the baby who is the reason I have come to this springtime knowing that, even when night is darkest, somewhere a nightingale sings.

Now, Nina is singing softly as she rises and falls through air. I grab her feet and she giggles, then sings again. "How 'bout a walk?" I ask, and she raises her arms to mine. "Hokay!" I sweep her to the ground and start to chant, "Walking, walking, walking, walking," caring little if anybody hears. "Waa, waa, waa, waa," Nina joins me, bobbing her head to the beat, and, hand in hand, we head slowly across the grass. A little wobbly, maybe. But we're standing.

Jill Riddell

INFINITY UNPLUGGED

My father is a scientist, and though his professional pursuit as a petroleum geologist is to find out what's under the ground, he also takes an interest in what's on and above it. On summer nights when we grew tired of TV our family would soak itself in mosquito repellent and settle onto lawn chairs to try to learn the stars together.

We had a telescope. I can't remember any of its features except that the tube was blue and I could never see anything through it. Recently my dad confessed that he couldn't either, and it turns out we're not alone: Cheap telescopes probably turn more people off of astronomy than almost anything else. They're tedious to focus, and as soon as you do, the slightest breeze knocks it off the mark and you have to start the process all over again. So we mostly depended on our bare eyes to navigate the universe.

It's hard for me to grasp my bearings in a new place unless I'm the one holding the map. This was true for the night skies as well; unless I looked at the chart and found constellations on my own, I never knew what I was doing or what I was supposed to be looking at. I was a youngest child, accustomed to back seats and an absence of responsibility. So even with all the hours I spent under those spectacular skies, conscientiously nodding and saying yes, I saw Vega, the Pleiades, and Andromeda, the truth is most of the time I couldn't, didn't, or wouldn't. I wouldn't have recognized the Little Dipper if it dribbled on my head.

My adolescent ignorance seems like a waste of something wonderful to me now. But I didn't know that when I escaped Posey County, Indiana, I would be forever giving up darkness. This sacrifice never entered my mind. I was inexperienced enough in the ways of the urban world so that when I moved to Evanston, Illinois to go to college, I packed a flashlight. The first few evenings of freshman orientation, I stuck it in my pocket. I just didn't know that it would never get dark enough to need it.

The urban lighting systems that enable us to walk around without flashlights make living in the city like living under a translucent bubble. From our position, the sky looks like it's covered in an orangish-colored film through which we can see only the brightest of stars. This is because light from street lamps, homes, ballparks, and car dealerships shoots up into the sky where it encounters water vapor, dust and motes of pollution. Each piece of tiny debris reflects a minuscule amount of light, but altogether the effect is enormous. Essentially, Chicago and other cities shine a light into the atmosphere, and the atmosphere acts like a glass window that bounces it right back at us.

Until the use of electric lights became widespread in the early part of this century, every sighted person who ever lived on earth witnessed the spectacle of stars as a regular occurrence, something that could be depended upon on a cloudless night. (Gas street lights were around in England since the early eighteen hundreds, but they were much dimmer. And, until quite recently, street lights in many cities were turned off at midnight or earlier.)

Now I've lived almost as long under Chicago's cantaloupe-colored sky as I have under rich black heavens. And even though I love the city in a thousand ways, I will say this: I loathe the way it never grows dark. I suspect that never seeing the Milky Way anymore is damaging my integrity in some way I can't name. It makes me pettier, meaner—less of a human being than I was before.

I believe the diminishment I feel is related to the potential the night sky has to provide a person a grasp of infinity like nothing else visible to us on earth. For everyone living in urban America—and that's 79 percent of the U. S. population—our one chance to glimpse infinity has been obliterated. Even on a crystal clear night in Chicago, it's possible to count the visible stars. Which would number around two hundred at any given time. "Two hundred," a number I can count out loud to in seventy seconds, doesn't help me approach understanding of the infinite.

I see stars in the night sky perhaps fourteen nights out of the year, on occasions when I visit my family or vacation in wilderness. But it's not the same as viewing them on a regular basis. The damn galaxies just aren't there when I need them. They're not available when I pick up an issue of *Sky and Telescope* magazine and learn of some amazing celestial event in the universe that I'm going to miss. They aren't around when I'm feeling sorry for myself and need a reminder that my life is an insignificant speck in the universe. The stars are a feature in my life only in the way that mountains and oceans are: I have to travel to see them.

Of course, I'm among the lucky to witness them at all. I can only speculate on what it would be like to have never experienced the immensity of an unlit sky, the case for Chicagoans who never take trips to rural areas. During air-raid blackouts in the second World War, many Londoners saw the Milky Way for the first time in their lives. As a result of the blackouts, interest in astronomy increased dramatically in the city.

This is what I find strange about light pollution: It's the only serious environmental problem that's instantly reversible, yet it's impossible to think it'll ever be cured.

All it would take would be for every light to be turned off in the six-county Chicago metropolitan region at the same time and, suddenly, the stars in all their sparkling glory, would reappear.

I have this crazy notion about organizing a one-time, quarter-hour blackout so the kids in my neighborhood can see the stars. For a mere fifteen minutes, Commonwealth Edison could stop pumping energy out of its nuclear reactors and the state police could force all cars and trucks to halt and douse their headlights.

We'd have to call the blackout something with positive spin (Star-O-Rama, maybe, or Infinity Unplugged) and publicize it ahead of time. I can picture the moment so clearly: On the appointed night, people would climb out on fire escapes, open hatch doors to the roofs of apartment buildings, walk out into backyards. Teenagers would drive to open areas and linger on the hoods of cars; families would go to the lakefront parks as though it were Fourth of July. Everyone would stake out a space with a clear view and await the moment. Then, at ten thirty, when it was completely dark, but not so late that children couldn't stay up—poof! Commonwealth Edison would pull the plug and the glowing bubble that surrounds the city would dissolve.

The dark would descend instantaneously. For a few minutes, we would let our pupils dilate, growing accustomed to the inky absence of light. As our eyes adjusted, the stars would crackle into view. The two hundred we could see before would be joined by a thousand, then a thousand more—a sky swarming with constellations, clusters, nebulae, galaxies as far as the eye could see. And there we'd all be: Eight million people sitting in this metropolis on the black prairie with our heads tilted upward, beholding for the first time a sky that goes on forever.

Roz Warren

AUTO REPAIR

There's no place to go in Detroit that's half as fun as getting there. Especially in my daddy's Olds. The closest thing to heaven on earth is being on the freeway when Aretha comes on. I turn the volume up until the music is coming from inside me and go as fast as I can.

"What you want," sings Aretha, "baby I got." *

She's telling me to floor it.

I don't want you to think that I don't drive responsibly. I am a responsible driver. Responsible, but accelerated. I go to the community college, though I'm just seventeen, because I'm accelerated. I still live at home, though. So I can drive my daddy's Olds.

My father taught me to drive when I was fourteen. He took me to the parking lot at the Tel-Twelve Mall, told me to get behind the wheel, sat back in the passenger seat, and lit a cigar. "Do your worst, babe," he said.

He put on the country-western station. "Now I've got a gal that's sweet to me, but she ain't what she used to be," ** sang Earl Scruggs as we lurched around the lot. Dad slouched back in the reclining seat and gave me advice. "Don't squash that poodle, honey." "Watch out for the Winnebago." One morning he gave me a key ring with the keys to seventeen cars. "They're all yours, Mercy," he said. I gave him a bear hug and he smiled. "Sure wish your mom could see you now," he said.

Mom died when I was only two. She died in her car, a red Trans Am. Coming home from the supermarket one night, she was broadsided by a drunk car-door salesman in a Lincoln Continental. The car was totaled. She was killed instantly. The groceries in the trunk survived.

Dad didn't junk the car. He had it towed home. He rebuilt it. He wanted to salvage something, he says. Repairing the car made him feel better. He started collecting them. He buys wrecks and puts them back together again. It's like a hobby. He tells me it's therapy. "Auto repair—the poor man's analysis," he says. He must have over twenty cars now, plus junkers he keeps for parts.

Some of Dad's cars are stashed in friends' garages; some are out in our driveway or sitting in the backyard. We've got a peach-colored Studebaker down in the basement, because he took it apart in the driveway one summer and reassembled it down there, just to see if he could.

Everything in Detroit comes down to cars. If you don't work on the line like my dad, you work for a company that makes car-door handles or cruise controls. Or plastic saints for the dashboard. Or you're that company's lawyer, or the shrink the auto execs go to, or the funeral director that puts them all in the ground. Remember that guy who was buried sitting behind the wheel of his Caddy? He wasn't a Detroit man, but he had the right idea. Detroit is all auto showrooms, muffler shops, and intersections with a gas station on each comer. Motown babies are born groping for the steering wheel, and by the time a local kid is five she can call out the model and year of every car that drives by.

My dad never remarried. He's got girlfriends. He's got me. He's got reconstituted Chevys, Fords, Pontiacs, a Studebaker in the basement, and job security. He's got pals on the line to go drinking with.

When he gets too drunk to drive, he phones me from a bar and I drive out to get him. His friends help him into the backseat. He sits with his feet up and lights a cigar.

"Where to?" I ask.

"East of the sun, west of the moon," he'll say if he's really sloshed.

"Dad?"

"Anywhere you want, babe," he says. "It's all the same to me."

The streets around Detroit—long, wide roads under a big midwestern sky—are made for cruising. I'll drive down Woodward Avenue. We'll put the radio on or just sit quiet and watch the world go by. Woodward is the main drag—miles of glittering neon signs and fast-food stands. Everybody in this city learned to drive on this street. Sometimes we'll cruise all the way out to Dearborn to see Ford Motor Company World Headquarters, a complex of gleaming skyscrapers sitting all by itself in the middle of nowhere. Or downtown to the Detroit River to see the Renaissance Center, which was supposed to revitalize the inner city but didn't. Or to Canada, crossing through the tunnel under the river driving through sleepy downtown Windsor and returning across the Ambassador Bridge. I drive by my mom's cemetery. Over the entrance is a sign in lovely pink neon script—Roseview Cemetery—that I remember from way before I had any idea what it meant.

Eventually Dad falls asleep and I drive home.

I fell in love with Todd in his daddy's Eldorado.

My daddy didn't take to Todd at first. "He's too short for you," he said. "He looks like a hoodlum." Dad was wrong about that. Todd was a rich kid from Bloomfield Hills. He wore faded jeans and a beat-up leather jacket because it looked cool, not because he couldn't afford better. He had long dark hair, beautiful gray eyes, and loads of nervous energy, and he played lead guitar in the Clone Brothers, a local band. He was at our place watching television with a crowd of my friends. A girl I didn't like had brought him, so I started flirting with him.

I could sense Dad lurking by the front door later on as I walked Todd to his car. The girl he'd been with was long gone. Todd got into the Eldorado, and I leaned in the window of that gorgeous black car and kissed him. That's when I fell in love. Todd didn't seem too surprised—as if strange girls leaned in his car window and kissed him all the time.

"Call me," I said, dizzy.

We gazed into each other's eyes. Then he turned the key in the ignition and the engine blew up.

The next thing I know I'm sitting on our front lawn, with Todd and my father running around the car yelling instructions to each other, trying to get our old fire extinguisher to work and swatting at the burning Eldorado with blankets. A crowd of neighbors came out to cheer them on, but the Eldorado burned to a crisp.

Dad decided to like Todd then, either because he felt sorry for him or because he wanted his car for parts.

But Todd didn't phone. Maybe because our kiss had set his car on fire. I didn't see him again till months later. His band was playing at a bar out in Ypsilanti, and Dad went to see them without telling me. I guess he was getting sick of my moping around the house telling him how the love of my life had passed me by. Dad ended up having a pretty good time. After the last set, Todd drove my father home.

Todd rang the doorbell. It was late, and I came to the door in my pajamas. He was the last person I'd expected to see.

"Guess what?" Todd said.

I didn't have to guess—I could hear my daddy snoring away in the backseat of Todd's new Chevy.

"Let him rest," said Todd. He got out his guitar and I put on a bathrobe, and we sat on the warm hood of Todd's car, where he recycled all the love songs he'd written for his last girlfriend. Between the songs we kissed.

Hours later the car door opened and Dad stepped out. "What a night!" he said.

He squinted at us sitting there on the hood. I could tell he didn't really remember Todd's driving him home.

"Nice car," he said. "Is it ours?"

He circled the Chevy, patting the hood, stooping to admire the whitewalls, tracing the chrome with a fingertip. Finishing, he bowed to us and shuffled toward the house, still wrapped in the blanket I'd thrown over him. He looked like the drawing in my grade school civics textbook of Pontiac, the Indian chief for whom the city of Pontiac and later the car were named.

He paused on the front steps. "Call me if you need help putting any fires out," he said. ,

Todd phoned the next night.

"Want to come over?" he asked. He gave me directions to his house. It wasn't till I got there that I recognized the neighborhood, a posh subdivision that had gone up a few years back. When it was new, my friends and I used to cruise through and laugh at how grand and silly the houses were. They were all monsters, each flashier than the last. And Todd lived in the grandest one. It was a little castle, complete with three turrets, a (waterless) moat, and a fake drawbridge.

Todd met me at the door with a skinny girl with wild red curls and thick glasses. She looked about twelve.

"I'm baby-sitting," he said. "My parents are out of town. This is my sister, Gladys. She's a computer nerd."

"Computer hacker," Gladys corrected. "Want me to access your school records and change all your grades to A's?"

"They already are."

"Cool." She grinned. "If you're so smart, what are you doing with my brother?"

Todd gave her a friendly shove. "Come on," he said to me. He led me through the place, which looked like something out of a magazine, to his room, which was ten times the size of my room at home. Guitars and stereo equipment lined one wall, and his record collection took up half of another. I'd never seen anything like it. We sat down on his bed.

"Where are your parents?" I asked.

"Geneva." He sounded almost apologetic.

Silence.

"I missed you," he said finally. Then we started kissing, and I felt at home again even in that outlandish place.

We got to the point where if we'd been in a car, we'd have dusted ourselves off and gone to get coffee and talk someplace on Woodward. I'd never known anyone whose parents vanished to Geneva and left them a castle to hang out in. I wasn't entirely comfortable about it. I began wondering how I was going to get out of this. Did I really want to?

Then Todd stopped kissing me and looked into my eyes. I waited.

"Want to climb a tree?" he asked.

Climb? A tree?

"We have to take Gladys, though. I'm responsible for her."

"A tree?" I asked.

"You'll see," he said. "It'll be fun."

It was. The three of us drove to Ferndale, a small residential neighborhood. "We used to live here," said Todd as we cruised through the quiet streets. "Then Grandpa died and Mom inherited." We got out of the car at a sleepy little park. There was an old beech with thick, sprawling branches—perfect for climbing.

"This is my favorite place," Todd said when the three of us had climbed up to the top. We sat in the branches, looking out over the park and talking. When we ran out of things to say, Todd and Gladys sang me Elvis songs. I'd never been happier.

"And what have you been up to?" asked Dad when I got home.

Todd and I started going out. We usually took his car. I'd sit beside him, my head against his shoulder and the radio playing. He'd chain-smoke and we'd cruise and talk for hours. Or I'd just sit, quiet, feeling so happy I wanted to freeze the whole thing and stash it in a time capsule somewhere.

All this bliss made Dad a little nervous. "Don't get in over your head," he warned one night while he and I watched the Tigers pulverize the Red Sox on television.

"Too late," I said.

"He's a real nice kid," said Dad. "But he's got a few problems." I got a kick out of that. Dad spoke as if Todd were a faulty engine that needed a few days in the shop.

"What kind of problems?"

"You think that boy spends a tenth the time thinking about you that you spend thinking about him?"

"This is a relationship, Dad, not a see-saw. "

"Do you two ever talk about anything besides his music and his band and his plans? Ever talk about your plans?"

"I don't need to talk about my plans."

"That's not the point," he said, "and you know it."

Of course I knew it, though I wasn't going to tell him so. I wasn't stupid. I knew deep down that I was in love with Todd and that Todd was in love with me being in love with Todd. As neat and talented as he was, he was too insecure and unsure of himself to be able to focus on me. But that would change. I'd make it change. It was as if Dad could read my mind.

"That boy's a do-it-yourself model," he said. "You deserve a finished product."

I blew up at him. "I'm not one of your cars!" I said. "Don't try to take me apart and put me back the way you want."

He smiled. "Okay, honey," he said. "I'll back off. But maybe you'll listen to an expert." He took a folded-up piece of yellowed newspaper from his wallet and pushed it across the table to me. It was an old Ann Landers column about how to tell love from infatuation. I asked how long he'd been carrying it around.

"Five, six years," he said. "You never know when something like this could come in handy."

"I was only eleven when you clipped it?"

"Just thinking ahead," he said, rummaging around in his wallet. "The concerned single parent."

"The overprotective single parent," I said. "The nosy, interfering single parent." I told him I didn't give a hoot about what some old lady had to say five years ago about love. I was happier than I'd been ever with Todd. Dad would just have to trust me.

He kept poking around in his wallet. Finally he took out my mom's high school graduation photo and sighed. "You're the spitting image," he said. "On the outside. But on the inside you're just as pigheaded as your old man."

"I could do a lot worse," I said.

A few weeks later Todd and I were sitting in his car parked in our driveway, and Todd told me that he wanted to break it off. "It's getting too serious," he said.

I had the feeling that wasn't it at all. He'd found someone new to listen to his love songs. He just didn't have the nerve to tell me. I tried to joke.

"You want it to be more shallow?" I asked.

He stared at me, looking as if he were about to cry. I could tell he wasn't enjoying this, and my heart went out to him. Then I realized that if I didn't stop myself, I'd end up comforting him for leaving me.

"Ann Landers tried to warn me about you," I said. I got out of the car, slammed the door, and went to my daddy's Olds, parked right behind Todd's Chevy. I started her up and began searching for a good radio station.

Todd came over and leaned in my window.

"Where're you going?" he asked. "You live here."

"East of the sun, west of the moon," I said.

"Can't we be friends?" he asked.

I was so angry I wanted to back up my daddy's Olds, floor her, and smash right into Todd's beautiful new car. You break my heart, I'll wreck your Chevy. But I'm my father's daughter—I couldn't do that to an innocent auto. Instead I found Stevie Wonder on the dial and took off with a squeal of tires. Todd ran after me, but I floored it until he was just a tiny dot in the rearview mirror.

The music was good. It carried me through our subdivision and the quiet side streets over to Telegraph Avenue. I decided to drive down Telegraph, past all the Mile Roads. Ten Mile Road, by the all-night kosher Dunkin' Donuts. Eleven Mile Road, by my old high school. Twelve Mile Road. All the lights were with me and I was cruising. I love this car, I was thinking. Nothing can get me in here. It's when you get out of your car that the trouble starts.

There was a groan from the backseat and my daddy's face appeared in the rear view. "Apparently a man can't take a little nap in his own Oldsmobile without getting hijacked?" he said.

"What on earth are you doing back there?" I asked.

"I was sleeping," he said. "It's usually real peaceful back here."

I glared at him. I didn't need this. Not now.

We rode a few minutes, silent. I could see it was funny. And I knew he loved me. Still, I had planned to drive for hours—a heart-broken blond racing down the freeway at night with tears in her eyes. A real American cliché.

Having Dad pop up in the backseat like that kind of ruined the picture.

"Are we headed anywhere in particular?" he asked a few miles later.

"Nope."

"Care to talk about it?"

I didn't really. I wanted to drive. Alone. I wanted to drive for miles and miles and dwell on my sorrow. But it was too late for that.

"There's a twenty-four-hour car wash out on Lone Pine Road," Dad said. "Your mom and I used to go there to talk. If we couldn't get things straightened out, we figured at least the car would get clean." He smiled. "We don't have to talk if you don't want to. But the car could use washing."

The most miserable night of my life and we're talking about whether the car needs washing.

Of course, on the other hand, the car did need washing. It couldn't hurt to wash the car. At the next intersection I turned toward Lone Pine Road, switched over to the country station, and gave the full weight of my foot to the accelerator. Dad leaned forward to squeeze my shoulder, then settled back in his seat, smiling. "No rush," he said. "We've got all night."

It wasn't that I stopped feeling sad. There was a heaviness in my chest that I knew would stay with me awhile. But as we cruised along, the idea of driving in the middle of the night to take a beat-up

Oldsmobile through a car wash for a heart to-heart talk with my old man didn't seem so bad.

Cinda Thompson

RECALLING PERSEPHONE

"How's my hair look?" The TV newscaster "live on the scene" practically snapped to attention in front of Demetrice.

Demetrice—byline Demi Matthews for the *Daily Herald*—took the time to nod at Dennis Charles from WFPD-TV. Fine, fine, he looked fine. She hoped she did, too. Not that anyone cared what a newspaper reporter looked like, much less bothered to read the whole scoop.

Demi had to pick her way through holes in the concrete parking lot while taking statements and making notes. The news at Garden Park Square, as always at this time of year, had to do with the pickets standing not quite directly under the red, white, and blue signs: No Picketing. No Distribution of Material Permitted.

The anchor with the two first names finished his commentary quickly, and, his camera crew already having filmed the various sound bites needed for the six o'clock news, hustled off in their van. Demetrice didn't blame them. It was chilly out here, the Riverview Inn across the street being only a promise of warmth. The clinic's glass door in an unobtrusive corner of the brick professional complex revealed to the public only a closed-off entry room, a green plant cascading to a carpeted floor. Cars whizzed by.

On one side of the dip in the parking lot stood an aged cleric with gray hair, glasses, and a stiff collar. Mostly women and a few men in their "Sunday best" stood behind him. One middle-aged woman clutched a baby doll without arms and with one leg missing, the doll's eyes blinking open and shut. The woman alternately hugged the baby doll to her belly, and then swung the doll up into the air by one plastic leg. *Very colorful,* Demi thought. But she never included her own thoughts in her stories.

The woman and doll faced "the other side"— both young and older women, a few professional men—on the other side of the parking lot. One woman's long hair streamed silver down her back, and she held up her sign like a beacon. Demi's photographer had fled, too, but not before she had seen to it first that both this supposed "wild woman" and the woman with the dismembered doll were photographed. One must be objective—the first and main lesson to every young reporter.

What no one must photograph, of course, was the girl, the one now being escorted by a man and a woman down the picket lines. Demi guessed the woman to be the girl's mother, because the older woman admonished the picketer who jumped out in front of them: "You have no right! You don't know what we've been through. You have no right to judge us!" Another picketer warned of eternal damnation, eternal regret, and a "gnashing of teeth."

Demi Matthews, though, couldn't keep her eyes off the girl in front of her—a teenager, obviously, young and thin, her face covered over with her coat, for heaven's sake. Demi's impression of the girl was "all elbows." Bony elbows and thin wrists, all loose and akimbo, flapping out from underneath a winter coat. A duckling, Demetrice thought, though she didn't write this language into her reporter's notes. A duckling not yet grown into a swan.

Demi would swear later that she'd heard the sound first—one sharp retort, followed by another—before she saw the coat collapse. And, of course, then, there'd been all kinds of sounds. All kinds of people shouting. Shouting and running. A police siren and an ambulance. Demi standing over the body, scribbling. Not a camera in sight. Damn! Just the pulsing red throb of light from the police car. Loosened hair spilling out over concrete.

What no one had dreamed of getting on tape before the incident was the stand of trees beyond the parking lot. The brittle limbs and the falling leaves. The hidden birds. Demetrice remembered later the shrieks from feathered bodies, suddenly flushed from the brush. The flap of wings across blue sky, scudding clouds. A mother who'd called out her daughter's name.

What everyone, including the shooter, had also missed was the doctor, the so-called "usual target," entering around the back and far side of the picketers. The shooter had not only missed, but "evidently panicked," police commented later. Panicked, or not had faith in whatever was being called God to guide the bullet. Demi also kept this opinion to herself as she scribbled. The police reported shortly thereafter that, having missed, the suspect claimed to have "accidentally" fired again. Meanwhile, a girl lay dead on the pavement, while a doctor came running.

"Shelley!" The girl's mother had practically insisted, "Use my daughter's name. Doesn't anyone care what they've done to my baby?" Demetrice had nodded. It was not she, of course, who was ever finally responsible for headlines, those labels that sold the *Daily Herald.* The "powers that be" discussed "publishing concerns" and decided such things, practically behind closed doors.

Shelley. As in the shells Demi had once held to her own ear as a child. As in sea shells washed up on the shore by water. A current a shell could not control, a current in which this child had not even been finally allowed to swim. A shell, just the skeleton of a shell-fish—the whisper of tides forever caught within bone.

Dateline/Morning/The Daily Herald:

Demi stood in the hallway, listening. The powers behind the door argued over this detail and that. They didn't know whether to sanitize the headline—ALLEGED MURDER AT LOCAL HEALTH CLINIC—or go for something even slightly "more sensational." Someone cracked: MURDER ALLEGED AT YET ANOTHER ABORTION CLINIC!

Clenching and unclenching her fists, listening to her own breath in a narrow hallway, Demi Matthews, "girl reporter," who had wanted to be a writer all her life, was haunted by all she could not say. Images her editor would only admonish her that she dare not write.

Shelley. A girl becoming only bone before Demi's eyes. Some called such a girl the mother of an unborn child. Others, a child herself, never now to become a woman.

"Shelley!" Demetrice could not stop hearing the cry. Surely all the seas of Mother Earth would finally scream.

The reporter could not stop picturing a cascade of scenes in her own mind's eye: the chill air, the broken pavement, bones bent sharp, then collapsing, all accompanied by a sudden flap of wings.

The writer could hear gulls calling.

Rochelle Distelheim

HOME MOVIES

July. July so hot whole families escape the prison of their apartments to sleep in Grant Park near the lake. Whole families asleep, defenseless, out on the grass, in the open, and nobody afraid.

It is 1935. Lindbergh is my mother's hero because he did what he said he would do. I stand on the front porch of our apartment and lean against the window, looking into the living room. I see my family sweating—my father, in an undershirt and wrinkled work pants; my mother, in a flowered housedress without the belt. I am seven years old and wearing puckered underpants. My sister, ten, has to wear a halter top with her puckered underpants. She is angry because I can go bare from the waist up.

We can't drive to Grant Park to sleep. We don't have a car. I put my mouth close to the window and say, very loud, "Use the Dodge!" They can't hear me, of course. Then I remember: We didn't buy the Dodge until 1945. With money my mother will earn during the war working in a defense plant—money for a new car, money for the bank account that will swell and then shrink when I go away to college. I want to wish the Dodge into our 1935 lives, but I don't know how. I want to offer them my Chevy, sitting in my driveway now. There is no way to reach them.

Hot is hottest of all for families who live on the top floor, under flat roofs. In apartments with tiny windows that decide not to open that day. Louis sleeps in the smallest room under the flat roof in 1935. Only three miles from my seven-year-old life. I cross streets and backyards and alleys to watch him sleep. I want to invite him to sleep on our front porch, invite his whole family. But he doesn't know me then. We won't marry for 17 years. We may pass on the street, sit in the same movie theater on Saturday afternoons, run in the same gravel park, swim in the same public pool. Or we may not. Nothing would signal to either of us if we should brush past one another. He is 12, handsome. I am still in puckered underpants.

I stand outside his bedroom window, listen to him sleep, restless, twisting in his cocoon of damp sheets. His alarm rings. He wakes up slowly. He still does. He takes his clothes from a hook next to the bed, and goes into the next room. "Make your bed!" I call to him through the window. He still doesn't.

My father-in-law gets up one morning the winter I am ten and tells his wife he has an itch that must be scratched in California. He doesn't have a job and the Depression is less depressing in California, in the sunshine, with oranges asking to be picked and mountains instead of streetcar tracks. She says, "Go. I'm staying. Me and the children."

He goes. Alone, without money or much language. He packs a cardboard suitcase and walks to the streetcar before it is light so he will not have to say good-bye to his children. He waits at the corner stop. I watch him in the weak circle of light from the street lamp: a not-young, not-old man who has already forgotten what it is he will never have. "Don't go," I say. "You'll be sorry." He ignores me. "How can the children eat if you leave them? Louis wants to be a lawyer. How will that work out without a father?" He isn't listening. He looks past my face and into the faces of people he hasn't met yet.

I try one last time. "You won't know your grandchildren if you go away." He will never know me anyhow. I will see him only once more, in his coffin. I will be carrying my first child. I am told that a pregnant woman must not look into an open coffin. It means bad luck. I look anyway, or how will I have a face to put to the memory of a man who is part of my husband, my children?

He knows he doesn't have to answer me. He gets on the red streetcar and rides alone to the Greyhound station downtown, where he waits five hours for the next bus west.

There is a postcard from California with a picture on it of Santa Claus, sweating in the sun, in front of Grauman's Chinese Theater. And another card, and then nothing for a long time. My mother-in-law takes in boarders to pay the rent. Louis moves out of his room and sleeps in a double bed with his two brothers. After school he delivers meat for the kosher butcher. He brings brisket and chickens wrapped in waxy brown paper to our back door. I love watching him, serious, patient, while my mother searches for exactly the right change in her black leather purse with the torn lining. He takes two pink-and-crystal aggies out of his pocket, closes one eye and turns them very slowly until they catch the sun. I see why I will love him.

This is the year I have whooping cough. I hear him at the back door and try to hold my breath so I won't cough until he has gone. I can't, and a cough sputters out. He shows no sign he has heard. It is a sound that has no connection to his life. Twenty years later he and I will take turns moving out of our sleep, summoned down cold halls by other childhood coughs.

This is the spring I sit up nights choking. The doctor says that the clean air from the lake will help me sleep. My father, exhausted from his rounds as a milkman, naps for a half hour after his supper, then drives me to the lake in his brother's new blue Essex. We sit in the car, alone together on the deserted pier, through the long city night. We can hear the water. I sleep sitting up. My father plays the radio softly to stay awake so he can watch me. In the morning, before six o'clock, we go to Thompson's Cafeteria on Michigan Avenue for breakfast. We are the first customers. I bite into my toast and cough. I cough so hard I spit my juice and my toast all over the floor. My father takes a blue handkerchief out of his pocket and wipes my face. I am crying because the man and woman in white uniforms standing behind the counter are watching. My father kisses my cheek and asks the manager for a broom and dustpan.

My mother-in-law is wheeling a baby buggy down the summer street. It is 1940. I watch her from the corner. "You don't have a baby anymore," I say to her when she passes. I follow just behind her on her right so I can see into the buggy. I see a pink blanket and the tip of a baby's bonnet. I can't see the baby's face. She is walking faster now and looks over her shoulder with frightened eyes. She stops in front of a grocery store, opens the door, pushes the buggy through. A man comes out from behind the counter and wipes his hands on his dirty apron. He steps to the door and looks out, first in one direction and then in the other. He tells her that nobody is following her.

My mother-in-law folds the pink blanket back and lifts something very heavy out of the buggy. It is a half-gallon crockery jug. The man takes it from her and hands her a one-dollar bill. He puts the jug on the floor behind the counter. She looks at the dollar bill for a moment, folds it in half and puts it inside the front of her cotton dress. Then she leaves quickly, almost bumping my leg with the wheel of the buggy. I wait and watch the grocer pour a brown liquid from the jug into a paper cup, then drink. He smacks his lips and looks satisfied. Schnapps!

Years later, sitting over Passover wine at Seders—long after she is dead—her children will tell my children how she made whisky in a washtub and sold it to buy them food. I have questions to ask this woman in whose womb Louis gathered the strength to become who he is. But when I am young, there is never enough time; when I am old enough to understand how important it is to ask her, she has gone, taking her answers with her.

We can go to the lake now any time we want to. We can walk there, we live so close. Summer mornings, when the girls are home, I fix sandwiches and we walk together through streets shaded by oaks and dogwood. It's an easy walk, a beautiful one.

Usually the streets are empty on these hot summer days. And quiet. It's a quiet that leaves room for me to hear other street sounds, sounds happening very far away, in the city, where the lake washes past concrete sidewalks and thirsting lawns. I hear a fire siren; a stick banging against a garbage can; hot, cranky children, cramped in their sticky bodies; women arguing on front stoops. Then it's quiet again. And that's when I can hear behind me the lagging footsteps of a little girl. When I turn around very quickly, sometimes I can see her in her puckered underpants.

Shobha Sharma

INCIDENT AT THE DEKALB OASIS

The traffic was moving slowly on the Eisenhower. Even slower than normal, because of the snow and slush.

Eyes in front, look at your mirrors on both sides and in front of you and keep your distance from the car ahead of you.

From somewhere in the distant past Sharda could hear the voice of her driving instructor. How many years had passed here! How much had happened! Her goal was to get to Moline by 10 tonight. Mira would be waiting for her. She had asked Sharda to leave immediately with her jewelry and important papers and to not look back. Not look back! Not look back, after twenty years?

Sharda had followed Mira's instructions implicitly up to that point, but all she could do as she drove was to think of the past. Was this the feeling that a drowning person experiences in the last moment? Well, she had been drowning.

The stormy weather reflected her emotions. She thought how sometimes life mirrored those melodramatic Indian movies she had seen as a child: The principal characters would be experiencing some intense emotional upheaval—maybe the servant in the house was really her mother or the one rival in the company was really his twin brother separated at birth (What a bunch of idiots; couldn't they see the resemblance?)—and outside would be thunder and lightening. During the romantic scenes of boy chasing girl and girl coyly hiding behind trees, nature would cooperate very efficiently: Birds would chirp, the sun would shine and flowers would bloom all over.

Sharda was passing the building with the big red Bulls symbol. She remembered the year the Bulls had won the championship for the first time. Ramu had come home excited; he had tickets for one of the playoff games. She had never felt such enthusiasm, happiness and joy all in one single day. It had been very heady and made her think of something her father would say. "Be careful. Do not let your eyes stray away from the ground. You may trip and fall."

Stone Park? Where did people come up with these names for a city? Indian cities had names of politicians or saints and at least some sense to them. This was mindless, as mindless as the truck that whizzed past her, covering her side window with white spray. She tried to focus on the road and stop daydreaming.

Ah, this was better— the 294, I-88 split was ahead and the traffic was easing up. She put on her left signal and moved onto the road bound for Aurora. The slush and snow had been plowed into two big piles, one on each side of the highway. Sharda quickly glanced at the dashboard clock: 4:30. Yes, she would be in Moline by 10, easily, with a stop in-between.

Now she was close to the York Road Plaza in Oakbrook. She had a friend from school here, whom she had gone to visit six months back, for a party to celebrate Divali, the festival of lights. Sharda had been amazed by that suburb. You could drive for miles and not see a soul. Every house seemed fortified, reminding her of Lake Forest recreated in a hurry.

Her friend Radha lived in a mansion. To get to it they had to open these massive wrought iron gates with a password Radha had given them! Sharda had been almost speechless at the party, just soaking in the house, the opulence and the jewelry all around.

Her Oak Park friends were mortified if people from out of town or other parts of Illinois confused these two suburbs. How could Frank Lloyd Wright's historic district be confused with this new suburb's corporate buildings! To Sharda, it didn't really matter, because it was all the same. Both were far away from India.

Signs for the Morton Arboretum were coming up ahead. Sharda remembered Ramu taking her there in early fall one year. Though he did not care for gardening, he knew she spent her summer months outside, tending her garden, and he had made a special trip here as a birthday present.

He could be so thoughtful and loving. Was she doing the right thing now? Maybe this was all a big mistake. Should she turn back?

After all, Ramu had been the one who had taught her to be independent. She could drive anywhere she wanted. He had allowed her to go home to visit her folks every two to three years, and had worked with her in decorating their home. So what if he lost his temper once in a while?

But it was hard to forget what had followed at home that evening of her birthday: the dried flowers she had bought at the arboretum all over the kitchen floor, along with the broken glass bangles and her tears. Now her vision blurred as she wiped her eyes and for the hundredth time told herself that she was going the right way. She mumbled a prayer to the god Murugan to protect her, a little poem she had learnt from a friend at school. Every time that she walked home in the night or when she was afraid of her father coming home once again to yell and strike her mother, she would repeat this prayer. Somehow, it calmed her down and made her tasks more manageable.

How fitting—she could see that she was close to Aurora, which meant the Aurora temple was nearby. In her mind's eye she saw the red brick, carved, arched and majestic temple rising above the parking lot, bringing dignity, hope and salvation to the emigrant Hindu masses. To her it was an important landmark, not of isolation from the rest of America, but for a sense of belonging, being home, being with her people. Ramu was a non-believer, so he would not go there often, but she was free to visit the temple whenever she felt like it.

As she paid her toll near the Batavia-Aurora area, her stomach rumbled. When had she eaten? A hurried sandwich, whatever she could find in the refrigerator. Well, she should probably stop at DeKalb and get something. She remembered some fast food chain there, a McDonald's or Burger King, where she could pick up something vegetarian.

The highway narrowed a bit here and she could see signs that called this some kind of corridor for Illinois Science. Oh, yes, Fermi lab was close by. Years back, when she had been in college, for a presentation she had won a book containing notes by the great Enrico Fermi. Everybody had shown such reverence while browsing through it; as far as she was concerned it had been hard to decipher anything. For all she knew, it could have been some doodling-while-bored piece that some lab assistant found after Fermi died. Suddenly she realized how much she missed science. She had not been able to continue further studies after coming here with her degree in physics, for the university campus that she was considering had been so far away from her suburban home. So much had happened after this move closer to the city that she had no time to think of her career.

Well, she was lucky that she had no children. How horrible this would be for them! She had heard from a neighbor, Susan, who was a single parent, how much she had to talk to her twelve-year-old son when she had decided to leave her husband. The son had kept saying, "Why can't you work this out, Mom? I want a family, not two homes." Now he was almost twenty-five, away working. Now he understood, but it had been very trying.

In spite of all her own trials, Susan had been there for Sharda after every incident. She had been the one to persuade her to do something and not keep saying, "Things will get better; I know they will." Susan had given her books to read and urged her to go to certain group meetings. Sharda could not do the meeting part, but she read the books and kept telling herself, "These are books, not real life. Things will be better if only I work harder at this. After all, the easiest thing is to give up."

Signs for DeKalb were coming up. Funny how when you were dreaming time flew. Sharda craned her neck to see the oasis. Yes, it was right ahead. She put on her right turn signal, eased onto the exit ramp, and parked her car in the lot. Yes, it was a McDonald's. Okay, at least the French fries tasted better here. What a pain being a vegetarian; she always had to scrounge for protein.

There were a lot of people. Where were people going this time of year? The holidays were over. Didn't they have jobs or something? Sharda walked up to the cash counter, paid for her stuff and headed for her car.

But she couldn't spot her car. She had been preoccupied, had not made a mental note of whether she had parked close to the door or near a distinctive car or van. Sharda walked through the whole parking lot before she realized that her car could not be seen anywhere. A sinking feeling suddenly descended on her, like the time in India when she had left her passport and purse in a hotel and had stepped into a taxi without it, Panic overtook her. Her mind blanked and she began crying uncontrollably.

As she sobbed, all her fear and concern came pouring out in incoherent words. If anybody had heard her they would have assumed it was gibberish, because she was talking in her native tongue, Tamil. (Her friend Hema had said that during childbirth, as she screamed with pain, she herself did not speak in English but in Tamil.)

Sharda was oblivious to her surroundings, so she was startled when a woman's voice said, "Is anything the matter, dear?"

The woman, with horn-rimmed glasses and sonorous voice, looked and sounded like a college professor. Sharda quickly wiped her face and blurted out, "I'm having a horrible day and now I can't find my car!"

The woman looked at her as if she had said, "I can't find my brain," but she spoke calmly. "What kind of car is it?"

Sharda told her all she knew about the car. She kicked herself mentally for not taking more interest in cars all these years. After the two women did a thorough search once more, the stranger told Sharda to come inside to report the car missing.

Sharda was in a daze, but she had the presence of mind to thank her companion for helping her. "I'm so sorry I'm delaying you."

The woman said very graciously, "Nonsense, that's quite all right," and then she went up to the counter and told the man standing there about the car.

The man did not wait for all the details. He just jumped in the middle of her words to say, "Ma'am, did you go to the other parking lot? We have two entrances, one on the east side and the other on the west side. You may have entered through one door and exited through the other."

Sharda felt so foolish when she heard this. She thanked him profusely. The man gave a dry laugh and said, "Thank me after you find your car there, ma'am."

Sure enough, the car was on the other side. "Who would have thought of this? I have come to this place so many times and not noticed the two entrances!" said the stranger, as Sharda thanked her.

Then the woman asked Sharda, "You know it's none of my business, but...is there anything I can do for you? You know, I am really not in a hurry and we can have some coffee together. The food you bought will be too cold to eat by now. Come, let me buy you coffee."

Sharda remembered the clammy feeling in her hands and glanced at the cold fries. She felt funny to eat with a stranger, but somehow this woman did not seem like a stranger anymore. Sharda accepted. The woman, who said her name was Linda and that she was on her way to visit her son in the Quad Cities, went to get the coffee while Sharda looked for an empty table where she could sit down, where she could collect her thoughts before setting off.

Linda talked about her journey, her life and her son with ease. Sharda thought, *Some women talk so casually about their lives and issues. In India, you never talked about all this so freely. You were always afraid that your neighbors and friends would gossip around for days about something you said.* Even here, she had been too cautious to talk to her Indian friends, except for Mira, about personal problems. But with Linda she felt comfortable, and even blurted out the reason why she was on the road today.

Linda listened with concern and rapt attention. She sighed at the end and said, "Shaar-dah, take my card. If you ever need me, just call. In case your friend Mira wants an extra hand or piece of advice. It never hurts to tell. Don't feel you are alone in this."

Sharda was grateful. Yes, Mira did not have any experience with all this. She had listened to Sharda's story with shock and all she had said was to come and she would think of something.

Linda gave Sharda's hand a squeeze, wished her a safe journey, and left.

Sharda looked at her watch and realized with horror that the crazy events at the oasis had taken a big chunk of her time. She went hurriedly to the public phone, put in the money, and dialed Mira's number. Mira sounded worried. "Where are you? We are waiting for you." Sharda quickly explained the reason for the delay and got back to her car. As she got onto the highway, she puzzled over the "we" that Mira had used. And then she figured it out: Mira must be referring to Ashok, her husband.

Past DeKalb and Rochelle, I-88 danced and flirted with the Rock River all the way to Rock Falls. Sharda remembered the first time Ramu had taken her to visit Mira. They had confused Rock Falls with

Rock Island and Ramu had said, "We have made it in record time!" From Rock Falls to the Iowa border and Rock Island, where Mira lived, was a good one to one-and-a-half hours more of driving through sparsely populated land. Sharda was convinced that the overcrowding in India could be solved if land or people could just be moved around from here to there. It was not fair, all these empty stretches, all this land for fewer people.

The road got lonelier as she got closer to the Quad Cities. The John Deere plant loomed up ahead as the road curved and she knew she had just a few more miles left. Somehow the whole madness with the car seemed to revive and rejuvenate her. Linda seemed so nice. Sharda felt her card in her coat pocket. A new friend.

Sixteenth Street, 22nd Street, turn right. Yes, the house was there. Mira came running outside. Sharda parked and got out to hug Mira.

"Come in, come in," Mira cried out excitedly.

What's this? Ramu was there, grinning at her!

"Surprise, surprise! Happy 20th anniversary!" yelled Mira and Ashok in chorus. Mira added, "There's one more surprise, Sharda. I hope you brought your passport like I asked you to. We have arranged a trip to Canada for the two of you!"

Sharda's hand clutched the card in her pocket.

Patricia Cronin

MAEMAL'S HEART

You can't get lost driving from Chicago to Carrollton, Illinois; there's no simpler destination. Pick any day, setting aside five and a half hours. Drive south for four and a half; turn right. Go on for another sixty minutes until you see a sign boasting the town's population of 2,800. Cross over the railroad tracks of the city limits, so to speak, make a quick left turn—this would be before the grain elevators—and park in front of the Levee Tavern. Mention my name and the owner, my Uncle Joe, just might buy you a beer.

I find great comfort in directions, the reliability of arrivals, departures, calculating the miles traveled, tracing my index finger along major and minor arteries in a Rand McNally Atlas. Suddenly daily contradictions are diminished in size and threat, and I live the neat, uncomplicated existence of an algebraic equation: "$a + b^a = c^a$." True ecstasy, however, is knowing precisely where you want to go and how to get there, without the benefit of map or other cartographic recipe.

I'm haunted by life's resemblance to a pop quiz. Not because I refuse to do my homework, but for the absence of clear-cut answers. And so the drive to Carrollton gives me reassurance that life can be a steady, cheerful ride along a scenic path.

Arrival in that small city is another matter entirely, for there I become part of the larger country known as "family," and well-known borders shift. I'm no longer a single thread in a living tapestry, some familial work-in-progress. Instead, I belong to a tribe, surrounded by people who have the same last name as me. We're propelled by an ancient hunger for renewal, and bring to the circle our argots, superstitions, and family myths. We huddle closer fueled by rituals of celebration or mourning. But there is no ritual to address the reason why I drove here today. I have only come to visit Maemal.

Specifically, you do this: south on Interstate 55 for four and a half hours. Pack sandwiches and have one as you pass through Bolingbrook, since there's usually some kind of road construction going on. Clip past Braidwood, Dwight,

Odell, Lexington, McLean, Atlanta, and Lincoln. Begin to fall asleep at the wheel when you hit Springfield.

Attempt to spy the dome of the capital from the road as you're driving through—it's exactly at this one hilly stretch of I-55, past the sign for the airport, maybe two or three miles. You'll have to stretch your neck and focus over the treetops. But it's there. I've seen it.

I arrive at Maemal's empty house. Exhausted, I lie on her bed and study the ceiling fan. I wiggle into a more comfortable position, my arms spread away from my body, legs apart. I feel like that drawing by da Vinci: suspended, motionless. My backbone becomes rigid and in my mind's eye I trace each segment of my spine, but rather than vertebrae, I see the road signs for the different small towns I pass while on the interstate. Driving down I-55 is a lullaby that rocks me to sleep into some recurring dream. Each trip I am six years old and car sick; or ten, sandwiched between two older brothers in the back seat of a '65 green Buick. Or, I am thirty and traveling alone.

I stand in the kitchen trying to conjure up an olfactory memory of Maemal's fried chicken or sweet vinegar cole slaw, something that would architecturally support my own memories like beams and scaffolding. The house will remain empty until her children decide what to do with it. Until then, it serves as a guesthouse for vagabond granddaughters and the like.

The shelves and closets are mostly bare; a few photographs and knickknacks remain. The house is airy, not in the way that makes me think of spring, but of something vanished. While sitting at the kitchen table, I concentrate, sort through mental snapshots, deciding what's real. I get a blurred image of her sitting there, not at the head of the table where she should be, but off to the side somewhat, saving the place of honor for my father, her oldest son. I can recall only two other memories I possess for certain. The others have become family myth—part reality, part hearsay—growing larger than the original.

You'll drive past neat cornfields, growing in precise, ribbed rows and opening up like Japanese fans. Singular squares of farm land cut into the earth resemble old Polaroid snapshots and document years of family and work and prayers for good weather. Stare with suspicion at how the expanse of the flatlands distorts the size of perfectly red barns, populated with still and silent Holstein cows. Look to your right at the Amtrak rails running parallel and feel trapped in the enduring landscape, a scene built around some omnificent child's H-O train set.

Once when I was seventeen, Maemal played the piano for me. I never knew she won a local music contest in high school. The melody was breezy, romping, though I can't recall the name of the piece. In an act of boldness or innocence—I can't tell even in retrospect—I asked if it was hard for her when Grandpa died, leaving her with seven kids to care for, alone. She kept playing, not missing a beat, "I was very busy, so I never really thought about it."

I believe I knew even then that it was a lie. While I don't think she spent nights sobbing, it's difficult to imagine her unaffected, despite her correct posture and stern warmth. Perhaps she didn't want me to worry or be afraid. And I have no idea what made me even ask such a personal question. But I did and I got the answer I expected, though I don't believe it was the truth.

Check your watch. If you left Chicago at 9:00 AM, about 1:30 you'll see a sign for Route 108 and off on the top of the hill there's the Country Kitchen Restaurant. Great cherry pie. Turn right onto 108. The two-lane road passes over veiny little rivers such as Taylor Creek and the Little Joe, often dried up like death itself. Just past Carlinville—the big town east of Carrollton—about a half mile out, but still proceeding on 108, gas up and pee at the Mobil station on the left hand side of the road. Directly across the street is a Dairy Queen. Right about this time a Peanut Buster Parfait is not out of order.

The summer I turned nine, my cousin Bertram Lee and I spent our entire vacation exploring Maemal's sewing kit. I recall watching her for stretches at a time while she mended my Uncle's shirts or worked on her quilts. When she was finished, we'd rifle through her supplies. Bertie liked to play with the pinking shears and button holer. I preferred piecing together scraps of fabric, matching the colors with different buttons. Our enthusiasm usually left the sewing kit in mighty disarray, so that Maemal was forced to hide it or otherwise place it out of reach. The delight we took in this game was Jupiterian, so, while it did take us some time to unearth the sewing basket, ultimately we found it.

Once, as Bertie balanced on a dictionary atop Maemal's rocking chair, reaching up into her closet to take down the basket, he began picking out her pin cushions: a tomato, strawberry, and the last one—heart-shaped and completely filled with pins. He dangled it in front of my face menacingly and said, "Look, Annie, *Maemal's* heart!"

Our humor has kept its darker shade and now the joke is, "If you want to visit everyone in the family, you need to make only two stops: the Levee and the nursing home."

In the front lobby of Mt. Gilead is a registry so that visitors may sign in. Like a wedding. Or a funeral. On Saturdays the local paper prints the week's comings and goings. The obligation has its fallout: some wait in the car, some drink at the tavern, some sign in but turn around and leave, or else rush by like amateur thieves, unable to force themselves to hesitate their steps, to stop even for a minute and say hello.

There was a time when Maemal knew my name with very little prompting. She would stare closely and smile, "You have your father's eyes." I used to take such recognition for granted—walking down a crowded street, the flow of traffic requiring adroit balance and pacing, and I'm stopped, interrupted by some familiar face, "Hey, what are you doing here?" As the rest of the pedestrians wash past, I have had one brief moment with an old friend. Something like that happens every day, anywhere. But it does not happen here anymore.

Technically speaking, you can choose from two routes. It's just that I don't take this way anymore: I-55 south, Route 36 west, south on 67, and south again when it turns into 267. That will take you right past my Aunt and Uncle's old house. The basketball net still hangs on the garage, and maybe you can even see the paint chipped off it. But since they split up I don't like to go that way anymore.

It happened slowly, of course. It often does. Years would pass and I could still eke out some faint, albeit brief recognition: "Oh yes, Bob's youngest," her head nodding, piecing together the fragments of names and places, but the information didn't adhere for very long. There was the usual difficulty of getting past the amenities of "How are you, Maemal?" Stupid question. She was old and failing and who knows how aware of it she was? Did she even try to reclaim some of her former spirit?

I don't recall when my family began talking about her in the past tense, the tense usually saved for the dead. I suppose it provided a more pleasant alternative than the daily reports from the nursing home: "She doesn't eat much;" "Nope, still quiet the whole time;" "She barely knows when I'm there." Besides, were there other choices—perfect, or simple past? A simple past, indeed.

We strain to understand it all. Aunt Dingo's theory is that her heart was big enough for all the pain and the good times. Her head, though, just couldn't take it anymore. My sister believes they can't help but fail, being in that home. She says, "There's nothing for them to do but get wheeled around and eat."

When I tell Bertie I'm going to visit Maemal, he asks, "What for?" Not in a way that's cruel, but neatly decisive, immune to the show of pointless duty. He tries to explain further: "Don't get me wrong, I love Maemal." Then, recalling perhaps the last time he did visit her, adds, "What's left of her, anyway. "

After the Peanut Buster Parfait in Carlinville, drive another 30 minutes and you'll see the following: a gravel driveway that leads to the local golf course, the Greene County Fairgrounds, the town sign welcoming you to Carrollton, the previously-mentioned railroad tracks, and my uncle's bar. Remember, if you pass those grain elevators you've gone right past the Levee. A Budweiser on tap costs you seventy-five cents.

In one photograph she stands solid, a true force to be reckoned with, easily twenty-plus years of school teaching behind her. No hint of award-winning piano contests or Sunday fried chicken here. Her dress is blue flowered print, buttoned down the front, fastened with a fabric belt, no-nonsense collar, short sleeves.

Sometimes when I wander the second-hand clothing shops I'll see one like it. I hold it up for inspection, and carry it throughout the store—not dragging it behind me on its hanger, or casually folding it in the crook of my arm. Instead, I drape it over both arms, like a fragile, colicky infant, careful not to disturb it. Each time I swear I'm going to buy the dress. Then, always, at the last minute, I say, "No, I don't think I'll take this one after all," and place it back in the soft, rumpled, boneless heap of other Maemal dresses.

You'll find the Dairy Bar at the northeast corner of the town square. It's a building the size of an area rug, like 9 X 11, but you can get anything you want there. It's amazing. There's a problem, though, with the way the plastic letters are arranged on the window, spelling out the menu. Certain words are formed too closely together, so if you're driving by the first time you'll think you can actually get "Baseball card pizza" and "taco sundaes."

Even today, saying her name is an invocation. We always called her "Maemal in Carrollton," as if there was more than one Maemal, and we had to distinguish between them all: Maemal in Carrollton, Maemal in West Palm Beach, Maemal in Prague.

One story dates back forty-plus years. My Aunt Dingo was getting married, and my Uncle Ted was quite sick at the time—tuberculosis. He knew he was ill and his fear and confusion led him to contract another malady, one my father calls "Irishman's Disease." Along with being afraid, Ted was embarrassed about his ill health and did not plan to attend his sister's wedding. Maemal would hear of no such thing, and assured Aunt Dingo, "He'll be there." Dingo expressed some doubt, mistaking Maemal's tone for simple hope rather than determination. Maemal repeated calmly, "Yes, he will. I'll make sure of it."

On the Friday before the wedding, Maemal visited the local taverns looking for her son, and, when she found him, climbed up on the neighboring barstool without so much as a glance and ordered a beer. Maemal quietly asked Ted if he would please come to his sister's wedding.

Uncle Ted sat quietly, unable to say "yes" or "no." After some time, he said, "I'll go if you do one thing—have another beer with me."

With that Maemal caught the bartender's eye, raised up two fingers, then flicked them down quickly: "Two here. Now! "

You'll want to make the complete pilgrimage: the house where Joe and Bernice first lived and Raney Park; the family pew at St. John's Church and Maemal's old house on Sycamore. The weeping willow in her back yard was perfect for playing Tarzan, and Suzie Bumbutt lived across the street. Visit the cemetery and walk slowly around the half-dozen stones belonging to you. Not many, by most standards, but you realize, anyway, "there are so few of us left." This is holy ground.

I'm trying to round up the past, corralling the stray memories of my cowgirl years, a period of time when I was an outlaw from my own family. I could always visit Maemal, though, and she would never ask the hard questions, just open me up a cold Pepsi. It's as though I want some proof of a life, of a past. But whose? I keep thinking if I make this trip often enough, other missing parts will come back to me. Until then, we look into each other's eyes, unable to piece together shared recollections.

Pushed toward me in a wheelchair is my sweet, shrinking grandmother, secured in by straps and a highchair-like table top. She is no longer held buoyant by the collective family adhesive, but off on a journey by herself. Some thieving entity has come in and stolen her away, bit by bit, silently extracting her inner mortar so that frail brick upon brick teeters for an indeterminate amount of time.

I look into my grandmother's face—her eyes red-rimmed, half closed. She no longer wears her glasses. Do the nurses think, "What's the point?" Inching nearer, I search for some sign of joy, or even pain, and discover instead that the otherwise clear border between life and death shows a nasty crevice.

I take her hand and lean over to whisper, "I love you very much, Maemal," and I'm surprised that she holds my hand so tightly in return. I'm happy for some response. She calls me "Johnny"—another one of her sons, an uncle I never knew—but I feel electric, nonetheless.

When I begin walking toward the door, one of the other residents, a woman I don't recognize, says, "I knew you were one of them. I knew you was a Quinn. You got that look." Yes, I nod, I am one of them.

You can usually make the ride back home in less time, or what feels like less time, anyway. For some reason, the roads don't look like inverse images of themselves, as you're sure they will. Just north of Pontiac, two-thirds of the way home, you'll pass under wires that reach across the highway, strung on Eiffel Tower-like telephone poles, and joke that you've driven too far, that you lost your way and accidentally ended up in Paris, or some other foreign city.

While my dreams play in color, my memories are held securely in black and white. Color snapshots yellow and fade, looking jaundiced; or, worse, the red tones rage clownish, out of control. But in black and white they are kept intact. I leave behind a sense of who I am, attached to me like a shadow, long and slim in late afternoon, stretching oblong, like an exclamation point, a bold truth.

I cherish those few things I own that were once hers: a deck of playing cards, a quilt, one hair comb. The memories I have of her, though, seem like the richest gift of all, a commodity that can be replenished, to some degree. My hand still feels warm from her grasp. I slowly close it, trying to keep tight this moment: an intangible prized possession, like Maemal's heart itself, placed high on a shelf, safe but accessible only with great effort.

Bonnie Ilyse Tunick

JEALOUS

For years, I've had a habit of recording my dreams.

Early in our marriage, when I mistakenly assumed my actions silly and cared about what David thought, I kept a small spiral notebook in my underwear drawer. Every morning, when I heard David's Olds back out of the driveway, I'd pull my spiral out from under my panties and recount my dream in vivid detail.

Today, I keep my dreams in a big red binder, categorized by separators, on my bedside table. During an active night, I am able to wake up several times and chronicle my dreams. I can fall right back to sleep and often wake up to read stories I scarcely remember.

The most interesting aspect of my dreams over the years has been their predictive value. For months before I gave birth to Eddie, my first born, I dreamed of billowy rainbow spinnakers, covered with numbers, skimming the waves of Lake Michigan. A mathematics prodigy, Eddie's a CPA, and he sails his sloop on weekends.

Before I had Sarah, a carbon copy of myself, I dreamed of a camera lens, its shutter reflexively opening and closing. When her kindergarten teacher declared her developmentally delayed and threatened to put her in the "slow" class, it struck me that she just needed glasses. Which, of course, she did.

Not particularly convincing? That was what I thought, until I dreamed of the canals in Venice closing off one-by-one the week before David had his heart attack. And, three years later, after months of dreaming that I was a flat-chested tomboy again, I learned that I required a radical mastectomy.

But, not to worry. I've been dreaming lately about the raspberry fruit filling in my birthday cake. The icing spells out "Happy 80th" at the top.

I've had one recurring dream from time-to-time that, uncharacteristically, leaves me perspiring and confused.

I am three years old. I am in a room with my mother, my Granny on my dad's side, and my Aunt Beatrice. They are sitting in big comfortable chairs, at different ends of the room, trying to get me to take a nap. As I walk in a circle past each of them, they pat their sturdy legs or abundant bosoms and, with outstretched arms, coax me.

"Come here, my angel," each one coos. "Come lie down in my lap."

I don't know what to do. As I head toward one, another calls me away. I end up walking in a circle, just out of any one's reach.

Sweet smiles fade, facial expressions harden, tones of voices grow stern. Soon they are screaming at each other.

"I am her mother. She should come to me."

"I am her old grandmother. I may not be around much longer."

"I am her aunt. I never get to see her."

I sneak out of the room, unnoticed, to take a nap on the living room couch, alone.

I always awaken from this dream wondering why, when I had my children, I was perfectly happy to hand them over to their grandmother or aunt. Or just about anyone willing to take them. Anyone who could give me a brief reprieve. Was I a disgrace to my matriarchy for my apparent failure to bond with my offspring? Did my lack of jealousy—my seeming lack of devotion—make me a bad mother? I wondered.

I've had another dream I'm sure must be related.

I am six and on the playground at recess. My daughter Sarah is six also, and my playmate, my best friend. We push each other on the swings, play hopscotch, and jump rope. We hold hands and skip and sing songs.

Suddenly, Aunt Beatrice shows up at the gate in her worn dress and old lady shoes. She waves and blows kisses in my direction and calls my name.

Everybody looks. I want to die. There is nowhere to hide.

I hang my head and walk slowly toward the gate, wishing she were a mirage. Aunt Beatrice has brought me a sweater, because it's chilly, and a glass of chocolate milk, covered with plastic wrap so it wouldn't spill on the sidewalk during the three long blocks she has walked to the school.

I reluctantly pull on the sweater and drink down the milk, all the while trying my hardest to disassociate myself, to give the other kids the impression I don't know who she is. I am not successful.

At the same time, Sarah sticks a goosebumpy hand in her pocket and pulls out a soggy wad of bubble gum she bought while waiting for the school bus, with the money her mother gave her for lunch.

I am jealous of her. She is jealous of me. Only Sarah waves good-bye to Aunt Beatrice when the school bell rings to summon us from recess.

When I wake from this dream, I kick myself for not having put more Twinkies into Sarah's lunch box. But I cannot make up for it now. It is too late. Sarah just turned 42.

My son and his wife, Margaret, learned early in their marriage that they couldn't make babies. So, they established a relationship with an adoption lawyer, and now they have a family. Three blond-haired, fair-skinned girls running circles around their Nana. (I'd never let them call me Granny.)

One day, Eddie informed me that Margaret was on a mission to find the children's birth mothers.

Incredulous, I confronted her. I never hesitate to interfere. "Why would you want to do that?" I exclaimed.

"They're the girls' mothers," said Margaret. "It feels like something's missing."

I still could not comprehend. "What if you find them, and they want their children back?" I warned her. "You're risking the most precious gift you'll ever have."

Margaret sighed, as if I were the one who had stopped making sense. "I'm doing it for the children," she said.

I whimpered dramatically and tried to reason with her one last time. "What if they want to establish some kind of relationship with the girls? Wouldn't you be jealous?"

"I figure if a mother has the capacity to love more than one child," Margaret explained, with the wisdom of her generation, "then surely a child can love more than one mother."

I searched my dream diary for clues, but even my subconscious was too old-fashioned for this type of free thinking.

Years ago, when the girls were still babies, I dreamed that a stranger came to my door bringing me incredible news. The dream had yet to materialize. Perhaps the stranger would be a birth mother.

I still hoped the stranger would be Ed McMahon.

I started dreaming about Sarah skydiving a few months before she announced her divorce.

"How did you know?" she asked when, instead of commenting, I bit my lip. "Another dream?"

"A mother knows," is all I would say.

Sarah moved back into her old room and grew depressed. I felt that I should do something, but I didn't know what. I brought home a box of Twinkies, but she wouldn't go near the stuff.

After weeks of Sarah's moping, I started feeling sorry for myself. When she wasn't working, she locked herself in her room. She didn't want to talk. I brought her dinner, but she wouldn't eat. Not like her mother; when down in the dumps, I eat my way out of depression. Mostly chocolate chip cookies and barbecue potato chips. Not recommended if you're at all concerned about your figure, but, at my advanced stage of body disassociation, it works for me.

One night, I lugged my large creaky body down the basement steps, battling cobwebs and moving boxes until I found what I was looking for. I pulled out a stiff yellowed coloring book that I had wrapped in plastic years ago. The cover asked, "What Do You Want To Be When You Grow Up?" Sarah had colored every picture neatly within the lines. The captions read: "I can be a fireman." "I can be a doctor."

I took the coloring book back upstairs and carefully tore out the pictures. I taped them all over the walls, over photographs, on the doors. The next morning, when Sarah emerged from her room to get ready for work, I heard her laugh for the first time in a long while.

That night, we ate dinner together, and she talked about her day at the office. Sarah moved into her own apartment several weeks ago, decorating the walls in early coloring book.

Last night, I had the dream about my nap again. But this time it was different. I was still three years old, and my mother, Granny and Aunt Beatrice were still trying to get me to take a nap. But, this time, they sat together side-by-side in a line on the couch.

And I laid across all of them and fell fast asleep.

Tamara Sellman

PASSAGE INTO NO MAN'S LAND

CHICAGO.

The elaborate book on the rental truck dashboard brimmed with glossy color pictures of the city Lucy'd lose her sister to in the short space of hours. Her dry eyes stung from lack of sleep; she challenged vertigo with deep breaths, last night's alcohol lingering in her blood. The bang and rattle in the truck's enclosed bed came from Luisa, who packed away things Mama seemed willing to part with. Inside the house trailer, Lucy knew their childhood friend, Maggie, was clinging to the hide-a-bed, pregnant nearly to term and likely exhausted from last night's send-off, which hadn't ended until nearly four in the morning. The poor mother-to-be'd thrown up in the car on the way home from the tavern. Lucy hoped it didn't mean Maggie'd go into labor soon; if that happened, she knew there'd be no chance Luisa would ever hit the road. Not with yet another option to keep her here in Salish.

Lucy turned the volume in her hands, smelled its new-book smell, fingered the hard edges under its slick jacket, heard the spine crack as she opened it. She couldn't know whether to trust such a book, with its glorious depictions of happy people, brave industries, ethnic festivities like so many other social studies books brimming with lies. On the book's jacket, a spire poking through clouds turned out to be the Sears Tower, "the world's tallest building," she read from the inside caption. Toying with an earring, she further scanned the text.

> "... this city of big shoulders...dynamic politics as fiery and complex as any metropolis could boast...a town as broad as it is high, with every road leading to the self-styled promised land of the Great American Midwest...."

She frowned. How would Luisa fit into all this?

"Hey, I need a hand back here!" her sister called out. Lucy tossed down the book.

Mama'd bequeathed to Luisa the dining room table, the only real wood furniture the O'Neill's had ever owned.

"Wow, she gave you this?" Lucy ran her fingers lovingly across the tabletop's faded lacquer, tracing with awe the memories of meals taken there over the years. Of birthday cakes and mourning casseroles. Late-night bowls of ice-milk-and-chocolate-syrup soup. Mama's wild berry jam. Daddy's filbert fudge, the nuts stolen from southern Oregon orchards during his fall migrations. Frybread dipped in sugar syrup, the classic treat when cousins came around. "Cool. This is really cool of her."

"You don't mind me taking it, do you?" A delicate, hushed concern.

Lucy blinked, smiled. "Are you kidding? You're gonna need this to remember us by."

Her sister smiled back, clearly relieved. The two struggled the heavy table into the truck, then wrapped it in quilted pads where it rubbed against the walls and boxes they'd wedged it against.

"So you checked out that book on Chicago?" Luisa brushed her hands together.

Lucy nodded. "You're gonna miss us, Lu."

Her sister looked back, her face long. "It's a whole new place."

"On the map, it's like a big red dot that stands for a dozen Seattles."

"I know. But what choice do I have?"

"You could stay, but then we'd all be disappointed, you being the good twin and all." Lucy yawned, tried not to seem too disturbed by her recollection of last night's ladies' room conversation with Maggie.

It had started out as shitty small talk, though Lucy'd sensed an argument by the way Maggie'd clinched her by the elbow and dragged her into the ladies' room at the tavern. "Just listen."

Lucy stared at the way Maggie's boots poked out from under the stall door. It seemed her pregnant friend was forever using the bathroom.

"It's not easy for her, you know. Leaving."

Lucy rolled her eyes. "You think because I made her dance with me out there that I'm having a breakdown over her leaving? Can't a girl have a dance with her own twin sister?" Everyone—Mama, Daddy, Sammy down at the coffee shop, now Maggie—wanted to make a big deal out of their separation, how it was going to utterly destroy her. Lucy wished they would just lighten up. This whole move was Luisa's decision, after all.

"It's perfectly understandable, you wanting her to stay."

"Give me some credit, Magpie. I only want what she wants. And anyway, it's not like she won't fit in."

"Just because she's an Indian woman that can pass as White doesn't mean she will." Maggie emerged from the stall, smoothing her oversized flannel shirt over her belly. "I mean, I pass for Black, but that doesn't mean I want to." The toilet hissed a dwindling flush. "She's afraid to fail you. All of you."

Lucy shook her head at Maggie's unfairness. She recalled when they'd first become friends, how it had been Maggie who'd been leery about befriending Luisa, a White girl, until Lucy pointed out that they were twins, that it was just their coloring that made them different. And Maggie had replied: "Yeah? I'm Nigger, Chehalis and Port-a-gee, but 'least I look it." Despite fifteen years of friendship, Lucy could never quite forgive Maggie her judgments that day.

Up to this point, Luisa hadn't shared any misgivings about the move. At least not with Lucy. She seemed confident in her decision to take the public relations job with that global corporation in Chicago. Happy to be able to put her hard-earned education to work. Pleased to be making real money for a change. The concept of working for both a salary and benefits was something new for the O'Neill family. If anything, Luisa seemed proud to be taking the family name to a higher plane. Lucy knew she would never have her sister's potential. Though she made plenty of money stringing Indian beads, there was no stability in that sort of work. Maybe this was what bugged Maggie, these pastures so much greener than her own.

Maggie took a long time washing her hands. "Behind Luisa's pride hide the hesitations of any self-respecting Chukwinninuk Indian."

"What do you mean? Everything seems to be going her way." Lucy was incredulous. Why was Maggie making this into an Indian thing? Admittedly, Lucy grieved that her beloved sister would soon be thousands of miles away, maybe permanently. But that was family love talking, not some blood-tinged political agenda.

Maggie persisted. "In her eyes, Lucy, the world comes crashing down if she fails. Around us all." Ca-thunk, ca-thunk, the hand towel dispenser pumped out brown sheets which Maggie tore away. She dried her hands.

Lucy sighed, regarded the fullness in her friend's midsection. "Looking pretty pregnant there, Magpie." She lit a cigarette, waved the smoke toward a cracked window in deference to Maggie's condition.

"You don't get it, do you?"

When Lucy reached to pat her belly, Maggie stepped back, shaking her head.

"What's to get?" A cold finger of night air crept into the bathroom, raising goosebumps on Lucy's skin.

"College in Seattle scared the shit out of her, Lucy! And now Chicago? It's like a dozen Seattles!"

Lucy inhaled, shrugged. "Luisa made it through just fine. And she never told me anything about Seattle except how fun it was." A half-truth, at best.

"She sent you letters on bar napkins." Maggie's eyes narrowed. "Lucy, don't deny it. I know."

Lucy frowned against persistent chills. It bothered her that Maggie'd found out about Luisa's desperate, homesick letters. Indeed, there were few intimacies left between the twins that their friend hadn't eventually become aware of over the years. "What's your point?"

"You never wrote her back!" Maggie rolled her eyes. "God, Luce, do I have to spell it out for you? They were bar napkins! Bar? As in drinking? Drunk? Drunken fucking Indians?" She poked a pick through her fluffy hair, smeared on coral lipstick, pulled together her purse with a frantic snap. "You know, Luce, you aren't the only one losing here!" Maggie pushed open the ladies' room door. "She's losing half her soul, too."

As the door swung to, Lucy trembled against Maggie's antagonisms, yet questioned whether Maggie might be right. That by taking this trip, Luisa might be risking them all.

Luisa rolled her sea-green eyes, snickered at her sister. "Let's just get one thing clear. I'm not the good twin." She shook her head. "As if." In her sister's tired eyes, Lucy perceived a curious light.

Luisa stepped off the truck, dusted off her hands. "I'm the poker chip," she said. "Mama and Daddy put me down for five and got fifty K. I'm all commodity. But you? You're the one who's the safe bet. The good twin." She chuckled.

Lucy looked away, rejecting the attention.

Luisa sighed. "You may not think you're much of an Indian, cuz, but you've got the richest red blood I've seen in a long time." She walked over to some stacked boxes next to her sister. "You have the fightback in you. The fury. The shining black hair." She leaned over, tugged at one of Lucy's dark strands.

"Yeah. The curse."

"What curse? You can't fail." Luisa grunted while she and Lucy hoisted a box into the truck, then shoved it along the floor as far back as they could reach. "You'll never accept things. Not like me."

"But I accept things all the time!" Lucy argued. "I accept living here at home. I accept that I'll never amount to a pile of shit, even if you will. I've accepted these things my whole life."

"You don't accept assimilation."

Lucy paused to think. Certainly she hated the idea that she should try to be more White, but mostly because she knew the world wasn't blind, it would see her brownness—had already seen it—and would always respond to assumptions that came of being labeled an Indian. And yet, she could barely relate to those with whom she shared generations of roots. Cousins, friends, all of them more interested in things far flung to the past, things they couldn't change. Even Mama was relentless in her quest for ethnic identity. "I'm not sure what you mean. Luisa, I don't know a single traditional dance. A single song. A single word. I'm as fake as any."

"You make great beadwork, Luce."

It was true. Lucy's jewelry always sold well at reservations, pow-wows, community festivals. But she'd never done it to please Mama, who had devoted her entire life to recapturing what she'd lost in a childhood endured at a private school for Indian children. And it wasn't to please Daddy, who, half Irish under all his Mexican brownness, lived yet to perpetuate stereotypes about Indians she knew she would never see deflated in her lifetime. Lucy'd taken up beadwork simply because she liked it, the creativity, the therapy, the escape.

"So where does that put me?"

"No Man's Land." Luisa's laugh sounded hollow coming from the interior of the truck's canopy.

Lucy recognized the knot in her throat and decided to leave. There wasn't anything left to pack that her sister couldn't handle herself. Without another word, she walked back to the truck's cab, lifted out the book, carried it to her Malibu. The car still hinted of the smell of vomit. Lucy wondered briefly about Maggie, then guessed that if she were in labor, they would have heard by now. She rolled down all the windows to allow in the morning breeze, and then she reopened the book.

The photograph was bright and colorful, of girls dancing in costumes. Their heads sprung with reddish braids, wreaths of tiny white flowers. They wore black velveteen dresses lifted underneath by lacy white underskirts; cinched around their slender waists were brilliant white aprons bedecked in embroidered finery. But what caught Lucy's attention were their feet, narrow things fitted into slender slippers. The girls seemed to flicker like rhymed flames in the space above the page, a frenetic mirage, dancing on stiff pointed toes, each exposed leg clad in pure white hose, each bent knee a perfect angle.

"South-side Irish girls celebrate St. Patrick's Day with Celtic dances and traditional costumes," read the caption. Irish girls. The auburn hair, the freckles, the clear green eyes. They were unmistakably Luisa's.

Goodbyes never took forever at the O'Neill homestead; Daddy's annual launch into early spring migrant work—this time to the Canal for picking asparagus and early peas—had taken all of ten minutes on the very same porch only two weeks before.

Luisa's exit, however, was a good two hours overdue by Lucy's reckoning. She waited till last, aggravating over what she'd say as Mama launched into weepy wailing; then it was Maggie, sniffling sincere, if weary, loyalties. At the moment the twins' eyes locked, the 11:30 lunch bell at the East Bend Cannery drilled across the bay. Lunchtime for their cousins, the oysterpickers.

Her sister wasn't yet crying, though her pale green eyes were puffy. "Are you awake enough to drive?" Lucy asked with practical concern. She knew Luisa well intended to make the Idaho-Montana border by nightfall. If she kept to the highway. If she strung herself out on coffee. If the passes weren't closed to late spring snow. If the truck's acceleration governor didn't kick in at fifty-five like the rental papers threatened. All conditions met, she'd make it.

Lucy knew better. Her sister'd never go so boldly. She'd stop a dozen times during the day to take a pee, to absorb the sights, to take inventory of those priceless things she was fast leaving behind for a $50,000 promise.

For all of Luisa's firm intentions, Lucy knew she'd always been skittish when doors opened for her. She'd even been late for classes her first day at the university, all because she'd spent too much time staring off into Lake Union fog, having become lost along the campus while wondering about the fog back home. Told in blue ink on a coffee shop napkin, this story had been the basis for the first letter Luisa had ever written to Lucy. A memory made indelible.

Luisa pointed at the open driver's door of the rental truck. "Mama's packed me coffee enough for the whole trip." She wrinkled her nose. "I'll be fine."

"Well, here, then." Lucy plucked a delicate string of lapis beads from her earlobe. "Take this for luck. It's not the Virgin Mary, but then again, you ain't no stinking Catholic."

Luisa slipped it into her own ear, chuckled, placed her hand on Lucy's shoulder.

Lucy drew a measured breath, clenched her teeth for courage. "If you ever feel lost, just remember there's only half of you. Half a Lu." She drew two slashes across her heart with her finger. "The rest of you is here, safe with me."

"I'll never be lost, Luce, and you'll never lose me."

Lucy shuddered at the force of her own tears. "What am I gonna do without you?" Her words swelled, ached.

Damn Chicago! It menaced like an evil temptress, stealing away her fondest treasure. Luisa. Her balance. Her guide. Her looking-glass for a quarter century. Without her, she feared the hungry, untethered vortex of No Man's Land, even though she'd only just realized its threat.

Luisa reached around and the two folded in a rocking embrace. "It's not like you think, Luce. You'll dance just fine without me."

Lucy sobbed, shook her head against the ache. Inhaling the fruity smell of her sister's freshly washed hair, Lucy surrendered a depth of sadness for warmer hopes built of beautiful aprons, pointed toes, red ringlets....By leaving for Chicago, she knew her sister'd fill a dancer's narrow slippers in ways Lucy knew she never could.

When the tail end of the yellow truck disappeared beyond the cedars lining Old Slash Road, Lucy instinctively snaked her arms around Maggie and Mama, holding them to her hips like a possessive mother would her needy children. They stood together, linked through the heart, until, after a time, Lucy cut them loose to their own grief.

Inside her back pocket, she pulled them out: messy, wrinkled napkins from last night's tavern, scented with stale beer. They ruffled in the breeze as she held them to her chest.

Lucy looked across their pathetic yard. The cold remains of last night's fire held vigil. She inhaled the scent of woodsmoke that Luisa'd soon miss. The canopy of spruce bordering the meadow...she'd miss it as well.

She found a ball-point pen buried behind the registration papers in the Malibu's glove box. The Malibu. She smiled. Her sister'd miss it, too, countless memories impregnating the car's mildewed cloth the way they hung embedded in the varnish of the dining room table.

"Dear Lu," she wrote, and when she penned the comma, the ball-point poked through the weakened tissue and bled blue onto her hand.

Gayle Brandeis

SUGAR RUSH

I used to think the Hancock Building in downtown Chicago was made of licorice. I thought that if you licked the black windows, the criss-crossed beams, long enough, they would dissolve into dark sugar onto your tongue. It was a miracle to me that the building didn't melt in the sun, especially since it was so close to it, being one of the tallest buildings in the world.

My mom once brought me to the top of the Hancock. I must have been about five. I thought I was going to die. The elevator was shaky, and I knew the licorice ropes that moved it up and down could snap at any moment. I wouldn't even go near the windows. Someone said that if you dropped a penny from all the way up there, it could go right through the skull of someone on the ground, and someone else said that if you jumped from the top of the building, you would die while you were still in the air. My brother went right to the edge and looked down, but I kept my back pressed against the wall. My body felt insignificant that high in the sky. Wisps of cloud drifted below us like cotton candy released from a paper cone.

When we got back down to the ground, I felt like I could keep going deeper and deeper into the sidewalk, like a penny dropped from a great height. I wanted to surround myself with soil.

That was around the time I started eating dirt. It drove my mom crazy. She said I would get ringworm. "Dulcie," she would say, "The dog goes doo doo out there. Do you want to get doo doo in your mouth?" I would shake my head and cram my mouth full of earth.

Around that time, I also ate sand, gravel, chalk, and soap. My pediatrician thought I might have anemia and prescribed a dark liquid iron supplement. I drank half the bottle and had to have my stomach pumped. I didn't have a mineral deficiency. It was just that everything I saw was sugar. I knew the world would taste sweet if I just ate enough of it. Once I got past the sour and the grit, I was sure I would find the nougat. My mom always stopped me before I reached it, though.

I saw buildings as confections long after I stopped eating everything in sight. I couldn't even look at the pink Edgewater building near the Outer Drive, it was so sickly sweet. But I loved the Bahai Temple in Wilmette. It reminded me of those Easter eggs crusted with sugar, with the little candy chicks inside. I once made the mistake of going inside the temple. I was expecting cherubs, marzipan, the Sistine chapel, but it was just a big tall room. The chairs set in rows were little better than the folding ones around our card table in the kitchen. It was like drinking grapefruit juice when you think there's a milkshake in your glass.

All this stuff went on even before the Hansel and Gretel headlines. I never read the articles until just a couple of years ago, when I looked them up in the microfilm archives at the library. I wasn't aware before then that at one time all of Chicago was trying to decide whether I was Gretel or the witch.

It was an accident. I was seven years old, and awkward. My big teeth were just starting to come in, and my mouth felt ragged and alien to me. I didn't talk much. Words were like sugar cubes that got stuck in my throat and dissolved before I could get the full flavor of them.

My brother was six. We looked like twins—I was ten months old when he was born, and he caught up with me in size by the time he was two. He used to tease me a lot. He was much more comfortable in the world than I.

We lived in a red brick building (cinnamon candy, it seemed to me) on the fourth floor. I was still afraid of heights then, and refused to go near the windows, even though we had a beautiful view of Lake Michigan. Sometimes my brother would push me towards the glass. I would close my eyes and prepare to die. Other times he dragged me onto our small balcony and I wet my pants. He had no problem with heights. He would stand on the planters and lean half his body over the wrought iron railing.

That's how it happened, really. My mom had asked us to take out the trash. There was a garbage chute in our hallway that led down to the incinerator. It was inside a little closet of a room that smelled like sour milk.

I was scared of the room. There was no light and my brother would pull the door closed behind us just to make me cry. I managed to wrestle the door back open, even though my hands were shaking, but I refused to open the heavy metal door of the chute. It pulled out, like the door on a corner mail box, but much bigger. Our huge trash bags slid right in.

My brother was showing off. He wasn't afraid of anything, he said. At that point, I was cowered into a little ball on the gummy floor. He stepped on my back and leaned his body over the open door. The next thing I knew, his feet weren't crushing my spine any more and he was screaming.

When my mom came running out of the apartment, I was still crouched on the floor.

"Where's your brother?" She grabbed my shoulders. I shrugged them.

"Where is he, Dulcie?" Her irises looked like blue gumballs.

She didn't even wait for the elevator. She ran down the cinder block stairway and banged on the landlord's door. He eventually turned off the incinerator and the police came to pull out what was left of my brother.

I've had dreams about my brother, and usually he is made of gingerbread in them. He is always as big as me in the dreams, even though he stopped growing when he was six, even though he is nothing but ashes now. Maybe now he is part of some grouper or sea glass or smelt, I don't know. I don't know what happens to ashes after you put them in water.

The parts of my brother that the police got out, my mom threw in the lake, right then, right across the street from our building. The police ran after her, yelling about evidence, the coroner, but my mom ran faster, my brother still smoking in her hands, and tossed him into that big body of water.

My mom was a suspect for a while after that, but in a rare moment of talkativeness for me—the words just popped out like Life Savers when you unroll the wrapper too fast—I confessed to everything. Not that there was anything to confess to. I explained it all, I should say. There were never any charges, but, like I said, the newspapers had a field day with me. My fifteen minutes of fame, although I was unaware of it at the time. If the whole thing happened today, I'm sure it would make a TV movie in about a week's time. Maybe not. Too gruesome, and no happy ending, although I guess they could end it with how I am still haunted by my brother in dreams, that my guilty conscience still gets the better of me. That's not necessarily how I see it, but that's how they'd see it. Hollywood likes those endings as much as the happy ones.

The dreams are pretty weird. Sometimes they are kind of like movies, but not like a movie ABC would show in some prime time slot, where kids could be watching. In most of the dreams, like I said, my brother is a cookie. But he can move like a real person, with elbows and hips and everything. Sometimes he flies out of the trash chute. Other times he walks out of the lake. Then there are times when he'll just be sitting on the little balcony of our old apartment, and rain makes his icing all runny or a bird pecks at his head. Once, he was raw gingerbread dough and he rolled over me, engulfed me like I was just another ingredient, like a bit of flour kneaded in. When I had those dreams as a kid, I would wake up starving. I usually had a big bowl of Count Chocula or Lucky Charms right away, just to get the molasses taste of the dream out of my mouth.

I dream about that apartment all the time, but of course, after the accident, we moved. My mother couldn't bring herself to go back into that trash closet. The apartment filled up with dirty garbage bags fast, because I didn't want to go throw them down that chute, either. Our place stank to high heaven. I tried to imagine the Hefty bags were full of gum drops or chocolate creams or even lemon heads, but it didn't work. Some neighbor complained about the smell and the landlord smashed down our door because he thought maybe someone else had been killed inside. I think he was a little bit disappointed to find me and my mom both alive amidst the smelly trash. He hauled out all the bags and my mom gave her notice right then.

We moved into a garage apartment behind a nice house that looked like peanut brittle on Sheridan Road in Evanston. My mom cleaned the house to pay for our rent. She met a man when she went to Dominicks to buy Windex one day, and she tried to have a baby with him, but it didn't work. She wanted a baby so bad, a boy baby. She wanted my brother to come back to her. The man lived with us for a while, all sneaky, so the people in the brittle house wouldn't know, but when he couldn't make a baby, my mom kicked him out.

There were a few more men after that, and a few more apartments, but no brother for me. My mom went to the doctor to find out if something was wrong with her plumbing, and she found out to her great shock that she had diabetes. She hadn't even had any of the symptoms, except maybe for peeing a lot. Of course, this suddenly meant no more sugar in the house. None at all. So I would stop after school at the little dime store down the street from my junior high with my friend Sonja, whose mom was trying to get her to lose weight. We would gorge on Now and Laters and Everlasting Gobstoppers and Nestle's $100,000 Bars before we walked home. I carried Handi Wipes in my back pack so there wouldn't be any telltale chocolate or pink sugar around our mouths or finger nails. We felt as sneaky and bad and kind of thrilled as if we had been smoking, or even worse, although we were too naive to know what anything worse might be. We were sugar junkies—that was bad enough—and I can remember racing home, sugar frantic in my blood, feeling like my bones were full of Pop Rocks.

My mom had a hard time giving up sweets. She bought dietetic hard candy, made out of fake sugar, but she said it had a weird flavor to it, like tin foil. Today, they make sugar-free everything—Popsicles, ice cream, all sorts of things—but back then, there wasn't so much. My mom lived on Tab, and she had a little plastic bottle of saccharine pellets that she put in her coffee. I tried one once, and it tasted like how I figure rat poison tastes, a promise of sweetness, but with something bitter underneath that can kill you.

When my mom first had to start injecting herself with insulin, she couldn't do it. She asked me if I would do it for her that first time, and I tried, but I was crying, and I put it in wrong, and gave her a bruise. I thought for sure I had killed her, the way she screamed. I dropped to the floor in a little ball, and the floor smelled like garbage. I screamed, too, and, for a long time, we were both screaming and crying and finally someone pounded on our door to make sure we were okay. My mom put on a cheery voice—she said something about primal screaming, some new fad—but then we both were quiet for a long time.

The hypodermic on the floor seemed to be filled with something other than insulin, seemed to take up much more space than it actually did. It was like suddenly my brother was there, inside that thin cylinder, the thinner needle, inside all the air molecules between me and my mother, all the words we hadn't spoken about him for so many years, suddenly there, thick as plasma, real as blood sugar. I almost said something, finally, but my mother picked up the needle, jabbed it deep into her thigh, and I was speechless again. My mom died seven years later—complications from the diabetes—and we still hadn't said a word about him.

If she were alive now, my mom would be a grandmother. My brother would be an uncle. When I was pregnant, I started craving weird things again—mud, laundry detergent, chalk. Pico, my OB called it. My body was screaming out for minerals, he said. I switched from Nestle's Crunch to Carnation Chocolate Chip Breakfast Bars because they have folic acid in them, copper, calcium, stuff like that. I couldn't get enough sugar. It was like my belly was one big sweet tooth.

When my son Cane was born, though, my friend Angelita brought almonds with blue sugar shells, like robin's eggs, but they looked like eyeballs to me, or glands, something that lived inside the body. The bubble gum cigars looked like blue severed limbs, or hypothermic penises, although I suppose those would be all shriveled small, not so hard and long. And when my boyfriend Russell pulled a heart shaped box of chocolates out from my hospital bag right after the placenta came out—he had stowed it in there when I wasn't looking—I tried to eat one, but the cherry cream filling oozed out like bloody pus or something, and I almost threw up. I haven't eaten anything sweet since then.

Sometimes, though, we'll drive by the Field Museum, Cane all bundled up in his car seat in back, and I'll think that building's meringue, or by Wrigley Field, I'll think mint. And whenever we pass the Hancock Building, I still worry that a chunk of that slick black sucrose will fall from the top, like a penny. I can just see it, gaining speed as it falls, screaming like an open Pez container, down, down, screaming down, slicing through my skull like a sugar rush.

Betty Diamond

FOOD FOR THOUGHT

Two women are in a kitchen. Woman #l is standing behind a table with a bowl of fruit and a cutting board on it. Woman #2 is seated. Woman #l holds up a large cucumber.

#1: I saw him last night. (She cuts the tip off the cucumber and places the rest on the cutting board.)

#2: (Peeling a banana) How'd it go?

#1: He says he loves me (delivers one chop to the cucumber) but he isn't "in love" with me (two chops to the cucumber).

#2: Oh.

#1: He doesn't see me as the person he wants to spend the rest of his life with (chop chop chop). He doesn't see us as partners (chops furiously).

#2: At least he has sex with you. Mine says he's in love with me, but he won't sleep with me (takes a bite out of the banana) because of his Catholic upbringing (bites banana). He thinks sex outside marriage is a sin! Can you believe that?

#1: Sex without love just doesn't do it (chop).

#2: Love without sex just doesn't do it (bites banana).

#1: This is not O.K.

#2: Sex through clothes is frustrating.

#1: It's time for me to move on.

#2: It's not satisfying.

#1: If you keep doing the same thing, you keep getting the same results. I need to do something different.

#2: Amen to that (bites banana).

#1 (Reaching into fruit bowl, speaking to #2 who is still chewing banana) Want an apple?

Patrice Clark Koelsch

THE PROMISE OF AMERICA

And if there is an afterlife? Evadne tries to shoo her thoughts away from this unexpected break in the fence line. You stay right here girl, she orders. You've got no business messing with that.

It's laying?(lying?) in bed all day that makes her thoughts so unruly, so sloppy she can't even remember basic grammar rules. Or spelling. To think she once won prizes for spelling and elocution. Penmanship, too. She'd been sorry to lose her lovely Palmer Method script to arthritis, but that was a failure of the body, pure and simple. Not something to be ashamed of. But it was mortifying to watch her mind go, too—all the names and birth dates and anniversaries. Evadne's a regular directory, Walter would announce at the Legion Hall. If St. Peter ever forgets a name or a birthday of anyone who ever lived in North Dakota, he can just ask Evadne.

And why shouldn't she know these things? And all the presidents and state capitols and every country in South America? Young people learned these things when she went to high school. At least she learned them. Peder Nilsen would tease her about it, would say she was going to study herself into being an old maid. He certainly didn't have much aptitude for books. So impatient with schooling, but so good with anything mechanical. Under all his foolishness he was kind, too, and clapped louder than anyone when she delivered her valedictory speech on "The Promise of America."

She can't remember exactly how that speech went now, but she can remember the girl she was then—her feelings, her convictions, even her shoes and blouses—more clearly than she can conjure up those jumbled middle years when she was Walt's wife and the mother of Arthur and Gerald and Raymond. It shocks her sometimes to see a scalloped-edged snapshot of herself with Walter and the boys. She doesn't recognize the clothes she has on, can't imagine how she got her hair to frame her face like that. Those were the busy times then. The only books she looked at were the ledgers in which she kept their accounts. And of course the boys school books. She'd liked that Raymond was such a reader, just like she'd been. Not Arthur and

Gerald, though. Both so full of secrets and wildness. She had to keep after them. Besides baking for the cafe. Waiting on people if Walter was shorthanded.

Folks here could take a few pointers from her about customer service. All she wanted now was a cup of black coffee and a piece of apple pie. A cigarette would be heaven. She didn't need a lecture from that dietitian downstairs. She's never been a big eater herself and she's never nagged at folks to eat. Not even the boys. What a person eats is a personal matter. No one, not even children, should be forced to eat something they don't want to. Of course this was not a view shared by Walter or any parent of her acquaintance back then. And here, where they were all supposedly adults—well, they shouldn't be bullied about what they would or wouldn't eat, either.

That was another thing she'd have to discuss with the new social worker if she ever decided to show up. Just when she finally got things straight with that Barbara Ferguson, she ups and takes a maternity leave. Not that she begrudges Barbara a break—good for her to have that baby and take some time to get used to keeping your wits about you twenty-fours hours a day—but the idea of breaking in a new social worker is tiresome. And she's not about to put up with any more visitations from that Reverend Mister-Know-It-All. Makes her blood boil, calling her "a pillar of the church." She was in the Ladies Aid purely for Walter's sake and the boys'. She went to the church the way she went to the dentist and the county fair and the town hall to vote. It was what folks did. Like burning your own trash and planting a vegetable garden. Who is he to tell her what her faith must mean to her now? A man of the cloth. A fool or a shyster.

It would have pained Walter to know she thinks this way. He was a sweet man. Decent. Hard-working, mostly. Treated her better than many would have. Some drinking men forced themselves on their wives, she was sure of it. Not Walter, though. Thought his ship was bound to come in someday. Even when he was sinking like a stone. He was happy to have the minister stop by, liked being prayed for on Sunday. What ever harm Walter did he surely never meant to do.

But isn't that true for most of us? Isn't ignorance the root of almost all evil? If we truly knew the hurtful consequences of our actions how could we do them? Arthur didn't know he was going to kill that woman when he took her home. She feels for the woman's husband and son, but she feels for Arthur, too. Maybe more. Unlucky in love, unlucky in life. Step on a crack you break your mother's back. Gerald's practically a recluse now, scared of her, scared of his own shadow, it seems.

But Raymond should be coming for a visit soon. He always brings flowers that just take your breath away and a carton of cigarettes and tape recorded books. He'll rub her hands and feet with lotion. Not many sons would want to do that, touch knobby old flesh and bone. Daughters are expected to, sometimes daughters-in-law. But Raymond's different. He's been the lucky one of her boys, and he's properly grateful for it. Never has forgotten what he's come from. If they needed money, Raymond would send something right away. Never looked down on anybody. Still, it chafed Arthur and Gerald, she was sure of it. Lucky Raymond. Just like in the Grimm fairy tales—the youngest brother is always the fortunate one, the one whose gentle nature wins him a castle full of riches. Also, Raymond had the courage to leave.

Seems people admired courage a lot more when she was growing up. Like in that poem she won the Fourth of July oratory prize for: "Barbara Frietchie." That was about courage, an old woman's courage.

Up from the meadows, rich with corn,
Clear in the cool September morn,
The clustered spires of Fredrick stand
Green-walled by the hills Maryland.

Round about them orchards sweep,
Apple and pear trees rooted deep,
Fair as a garden of the Lord
To the eyes of the famished rebel horde.

She can't get beyond the sing-song of this first stanza. She starts strong, then peters out. Why is it beginnings are practically indelible, while the rest fades away? Like "See the U. S. A....in your Chevrolet!

America's the greatest land of all...." That was from some television show. Ed Sullivan? Perry Como? She can't remember the program, only the sponsor's song. Back then you could understand what people were trying to sell. Now commercials are so jumpy and hard to follow, you can't tell whether they want you to buy hamburger or sporty shoes. When did catchy tunes go out of style? How did she miss that?

"Fair as a garden of the Lord...." Well just about anything looks good if you're hungry and weary. Folks would fuss over her biscuits, her custard pie. It was their way of being appreciative for the attention, for her efforts as much as it had anything to do with the actual food. She was an adequate cook—not bad, but not special, either. She'd always toted up her strengths and weaknesses with the same unsentimental eye she'd applied to the cafe ledger. Of course you wanted to come up with a positive balance, but there was nothing to be gained by fudging the accounts.

The garden of the Lord came with a snake in it. Booby-trapped, pure and simple. How could a good God let that happen? And why were Adam and Eve punished so terribly? She never could understand, not from the time she was a little girl. It just didn't seem right. Sure Walter and she made mistakes with the boys when they were growing up, but they never kept a loaded gun in the house, never cast their children out of their hearts because they disobeyed. And if Jesus truly was the Son of God, how could God let him suffer like that, nailed to a cross? It was like cutting off your nose to spite your face. Only worse. It never made any sense at all. She'd glance around during the communion service to see if anyone else might be harboring like-minded thoughts. If they did, they gave no indication.

Gerald's best friend was shot by his own father when they were out hunting.

"'Shoot if you must this old grey head,

But spare your country's flag, " she said.'

Old Barbara Frietchie wants Stonewall Jackson to shoot her instead of the Union Flag. A person's life for a piece of cloth. Man of the cloth. It could as easily have been Gerald who was killed that day. And that boy's father killed himself afterwards. Everybody said that was an accident, too, and the insurance company paid. But what people say and what people think is not always the same. Poor Arthur.

Stonewall Jackson didn't shoot Barbara Frietchie or the flag. Maybe he believed in heaven and hell. Maybe he just didn't see any point to it.

Like most things. When you get right down to it, there really is no point to most things. She was sure of it.

Mama was working in the garden. Not the garden of the Lord, just the garden behind the house. Papa went to town and took the boys. She wanted to go too, but Mama made her stay home to help. It was hot and windy all that summer. Snakes would come in the house just to get out of the sun. Her throat hurt all the time. Mama put Caroline down in the big rush basket Papa hung from the rafters. Caroline was such a crybaby, howling as if her heart would break, yelling as if the world were coming to an end. She could just reach up and pat the bottom of the basket. Mama told her to stay inside and rock Caroline a little if she woke up and started to fuss. Then she started to cry because her throat hurt and Papa went to town with the boys and it was so hot and she was afraid of the snakes, but Mama got real cross and told her not to act like a baby anymore—Caroline was the baby now. Mama said to stay inside while she was weeding in the garden. Caroline woke up and set to fussing, so she reached up and gave the basket a little push, like you'd push a little swing, but Caroline just kept on crying real loud and mean. So she got the broom and gave the basket a big swot to make Caroline stop.

She woke up to Mama screaming. Caroline had rolled over and smothered. Mama grabbed her and held her tight and blamed herself for what happened. She never told anyone ever her part in Caroline's death. That she killed her. Not even sweet Walt. "Suffer the little children to come unto me, for such is the Kingdom of Heaven." That's what they said when they buried Caroline.

What kind of a God would let children murder children? Would let mothers weep themselves blind and crazy? Would let fathers shoot their only sons? What kind of wickedness would deign to spare this old grey head but eat little children alive instead? And what would Caroline and Mama say to her now? That the point is there is no point? That's all an honest person ever really can say. There's been far too much grief already. It has to stop. Raymond is coming to give a speech tonight. Raymond's coming to hold her and tell them all about the promise of America.

Jess Wells

WOMEN WHO FISH

Rebecca sat in her aluminum boat staring into her tackle box, her big flat feet planted on the floor, her legs wide apart. She was aware that she had been staring for a long time into the dividers that cordoned the silver spinners from the plastic worms, the jig heads from the beetle spin bodies, the split tail trailers from the bobbers and the hooks. She was also aware of the ambulance parked at her house, its flashing red lights reflected on the water around her. Her husband was dead.

She should turn her boat around and go back, she knew, but she sat staring at the lures, knowing there was no point in her returning, and that there was plenty of time ahead of her to deal with the ambulance driver's pronouncement.

She had come home from grocery shopping and there he was, his head stuck in the goddamn oven, plastic bags taped to the side of the appliance. His big butt in its brown chinos was stuck up in the air. That's what happens when you're six feet tall and you die on your knees.

The ambulance turned off its lights, and, when the red reflection that had shown like blood all around her had disappeared, she reached into her tackle box and selected a silver spinner. She was in the middle of the lake, where people couldn't shout to her, where she would have plenty of warning if someone took a boat to fetch her.

She had dropped the bag of groceries in her arms, heard the jars break, called the ambulance and set off in her boat. She hadn't even turned off the gas, had she? Rebecca selected her best reel, her best rod, attached her lucky spinner, and cast with the elegant precision of a pro. Plenty of time for phone calls to relatives, for casket selection and service planning. Slowly reeling in her spinner, tugging at it to simulate a bug's dance, she knew that news of Floyd's death had already circled the lake and that people were watching her from their screened porches.

They would not be surprised that she had gone fishing; she fished every day, and, sometimes, if the weather was good, the fish biting or there was something difficult on her mind, she would go fishing several times a day. A rod, a reel and a boat are as good a way to cope as any.

Hell, she had gone fishing early in the morning on the day of her wedding, a day much like today, she thought. She had felt like an impostor then, and she felt like it now. That day, she had been all done up in a silly dress that she had let Floyd's sister pick out, and everybody had stood around with romance in their eyes. She had played her part all right, and today she would play it as well. Nice thing about being out in the lake is that no one could see that she was dry-eyed.

She just wasn't the blubbering sort. She wasn't the frilly dress sort, either. She was big. She wore jeans and boots and if someone complimented her on her hair she'd realize that she hadn't thought about it in months. She was a woods woman, a lake native, more apt to have pine sap on her hands than cologne on her wrists.

Her marriage to Floyd had been like a forestry project. During their courtship they had built a trout pond; they had spent hours at the hardware store, building, painting, sanding and tiling. She directed the projects, he hauled the heavy stuff. They had married, filled with enthusiasm for the yard, the house, the barn. In the evenings, they had sat quietly by the fire, Floyd working on an electrical switch or sharpening his tools, Rebecca sketching out the next day's project.

That's the way marriages worked, Rebecca thought, forlornly. In her mother's house, Sunday was the only day she had ever seen men and women together. The football or baseball or basketball announcer could be heard throughout the house while the men huddled in the den trying to prop their feet up at just the right level. The women sat on homemade cushions in straight-backed chairs in the kitchen. In Rebecca's house, even the food was divided: sandwiches and beer on the right side of the counter for the men, chocolate cake and gin on the other side for her women friends. When a woman entered the den, the men took their feet off the furniture, and a man in the kitchen made the women quickly look to see if the gin was too prominently displayed. No one left their appointed room without rehearsed entrance and exit lines.

One winter day shortly after her wedding, Rebecca had been sitting alone in her fishing shanty, staring at the blackness of the hole. The ice began to rumble and then the shanty quaked. She stepped outside and watched a woman bigger than her, bolder than her, step out of the cab of a truck. She had wedged her shed between Rebecca's and old man Robertson's beside her.

"Name's Zelda and I'm here to stay," she announced with her hands on her hips. With that, she shook hands all around the circle of men who had come out of their sheds to meet the interloper. When she grasped Rebecca's hand and deciphered through the plaid cap and thick jacket that there was another woman in the circle, she clung to her hand, grasping Rebecca's forearm. By the end of the season, the others joked that the two should cut doors between their sheds since they had spent the entire winter holed up together.

Zelda, a boisterous, imposing woman who was nearly six feet tall, with curly black hair, had joined the Sunday sporting festivities. Over coffee cake and rum, the women planned each other's gardens, each other's repair projects, and resolved before they left for the day to instruct their husbands to build gazebos or patios or new docks. The husbands didn't know of the advanced planning, even though they showed up at the hardware store or the feed yard at the same time. Unwilling to reveal where their orders had come from, each man acted as if the idea had been his own.

"What's so damn surprising?" Zelda crowed at Rebecca and the two other women in their group on one of her first visits. She paced the kitchen, gesturing with a cookie in her hand. "Of course we set our men's agenda. You get a man who can set his own, you get a tyrant. There's no other kind in this world, ladies." Cookie crumbs flew in all directions as she pontificated. "If a man has his own power, he's got the rest of the world telling him he should have yours, too, and that's a damn sight worse than what we've got here. So we set the task list, is that so bad?"

There would be no complaints from that crowd. Of the two other women in their coffee klatch, Deborah, after a first husband who had been bright, but beat her, chose for her second marriage a meek and dim-witted man who stayed in the den until he was called; Cynthia's husband was on the road selling most of the time and was treated like a handy-man when he came home. Zelda's husband was a big hairy hand that waved to them from above his leather arm chair when the women came into the house.

No one was beaten or bossed around and the women visited their friends and family as they chose. A couple of children got raised without incident. The lawns were cut and the shorelines reinforced, the roasts were laid out and the gazebos dotted their lawns. But there was a tension in the air, as if the women lived with a line drawn in the sand around themselves, demanding that their husbands not cross it. The men never did. Oh, they complained amongst themselves of being treated like children, and the women complained about being trapped in the role of their husband's mother. There was a loneliness in the arrangement.

"Face it, girls," Zelda had growled at them when the subject was broached, "we'd have married Styrofoam mannequins if we could get them to work." The women had shrieked in protest. But for years upon years, the task lists continued.

A few months ago, though, things changed for the group. Zelda's husband, who was more than 10 years older than the rest of their men, died of a heart attack. Despite what seemed to be Zelda's dismissal of her husband, she leaned on Rebecca's arm at the funeral, unable to walk without assistance, shaky and glassy-eyed.

"Zelda," Rebecca had whispered to her as she led Zelda to the car, "we'll share Floyd. We can still make plans. That doesn't change."

But it did change. Shortly afterward, Cynthia's husband died of a stroke on the train from Cincinnati. Suddenly, they were a planning group with very few resources.

Soon afterward, Floyd retired from the water company. For the first time in the years of their marriage, they looked around and discovered they had trimmed all the trees, fixed all the out buildings, used every inch of land for one scheme or another. The trout grew, the garden regenerated itself, the roof stayed impenetrable through the winter snows and the spring rains.

Without direction from the grieving Zelda, Rebecca had no directions for Floyd, just as Floyd had twice as much time and much more need for direction. He greeted her return in the evenings like a puppy, but the more he clung to her, the more she fished. Rebecca left Floyd still in bed in the mornings, without giving him a list of tasks or a goal for the day. She hooked her ice fishing shed onto the back of her truck and drove it onto the lake. Her shed was one of the last to be pulled off the lake and several of the locals took bets that the pick-up that hauled it would break through the ice and be lost. Immediately after the thaw, she launched her aluminum boat. Sometimes, from her perch on the lake, she would see Floyd wandering aimlessly over the lawn, picking at the heads of flowers, or inspecting the spotless drain pipes.

Today, Rebecca tossed her line out again, considered trying the shallows by the reeds.

Their planning group had lost two important members of the ranks: Cynthia and Zelda had begun the widow's club. They had paid their dues: these women had gone on the diet, worn the white dress, made the thousand Sunday sandwiches, and now they could do as they pleased. Callous, but true. They had the legitimacy of married women and the freedom of the single girl.

The group couldn't plan projects like before because there was no one to do them for Cynthia and Zelda. The two with living husbands had looked across the kitchen table at the widows as if across a huge divide.

Rebecca also had to admit that she had looked at them with some level of longing. For years, she had been planning the look of her life when Floyd was no longer there. She would travel, she had decided. She would take up running. She wouldn't eat beef or watch a single goddamn sporting event. The list wasn't important. What was important to her now was that she had thought about his death a thousand times without acknowledging it, and, in that sense, she had longed for it. She had plotted for it, then, hadn't she? She had taken away the thing he needed to live and dreamt of life after he died. Hadn't she killed him then? she wondered, so lost in her horror that she didn't notice the rod bending and the reel screaming as a fish took off with her line.

She reeled the fish in, a beautiful, shiny trout on the end of her line. She held the fish as it twisted in her hand, and she looked around her, puzzled. She was in the middle of the lake, not in the reeds where trout are usually found, and she was fishing with a lure for the top of the water.

The lake has turned over. Today's the day the lake turns over.

She had lived on this lake all her life and had only managed to fish it a few times on the day that it turned over. As fall turned to winter on this Michigan lake, the fish became more scarce, migrating to the bottom. Loon Lake froze to a depth of six feet, leaving twenty feet in the deepest part for the fish to live. In the spring, after the ice melted, the cold water on the top of the lake sunk to the bottom, while the warm water from the bottom of the lake rose, bringing the fish with it. All the fish would be in a jumble, the cold water fish with the warm water fish and the deep water fish with the shallow, and there would be just a few hours of fishing before they sorted themselves out.

She kicked open her tackle box with her foot, hauled out her stringer, and slipped the trout onto it. She hurriedly tossed the trout back into the water, secured the stringer to the side of the boat and cast. Again the lure was hit, the rod dipped and Rebecca reeled in a beauty, this time a bass that was lean and hungry from the winter's imprisonment in the twenty foot depth of water that remained unfrozen. Today, while the ambulance sat at her house waiting for her, Rebecca hauled the fish in, laughing triumphantly.

Rebecca filled her stringer and every bucket she had, and she was so busy that she didn't notice the approach of Zelda until her friend pulled up beside the boat and tied the two crafts together. Zelda slapped her hands on her knees as if making a pronouncement. Rebecca stopped what she was doing, looked out at the marsh-lands, down at her feet.

"There's no point in my being there," Rebecca said.

Zelda rubbed her chin with her knuckles.

"The worst part is, Zelda, I don't feel anything. And I don't think I can go back there and pretend that I do."

"I know," Zelda said quietly.

"I know it was never a marriage like on TV. Sometimes I'd watch those shows and I would just cry: who has that kind of love? But we were good friends. We were fairly decent companions." The women heard a splash near the boat.

"Christ, they're tryin' to jump in," Rebecca said, springing back to her fishing. She cast. "The lake has turned over."

"No shit?" Zelda said, suddenly alert. "Jesus, look at the fish you've got!"

Zelda reached under her seat, pulled her reel from its plastic sheath, hurriedly tied on a lure and cast. The fish bit instantly. "If we're over the limit we can just blame it on grief," Zelda laughed caustically.

Rebecca moaned. "Did I kill him, Zelda?" The two women stood in their boats, their reels in their hands, fingers poised on the handles of their reels.

"Sure, Rebecca, you killed him. And the water company killed him by retiring him, and the sports magazines killed him by telling him he was too old. I killed Stanley when I cut him off from pastrami sandwiches and he killed me when he wouldn't let my sister stay with us any more. That's what ya do. Some call it compromise. Floyd just wasn't willing to compromise anymore."

"But I saw him wandering around and I didn't do anything about it. We were the planning committee, Zelda. It was our job."

"He killed you, too, you know. You wanted to go to Europe but didn't want to drag him along and explain everything to him. Well, he killed that dream in you, Rebecca. You wanted to be a forest ranger, for Christ sake, but you pruned the trees in your backyard. Imagine how much you would have died if he had been any more powerful than he was! Did Floyd actually say that he was that miserable?"

"I had no idea."

"Just like him, don't you think?" Zelda said, hauling in another bass.

Rebecca gritted her teeth. In fact, Floyd had become more and more withdrawn over the years, until he wouldn't select a movie, couldn't choose between chicken or beef for dinner. "Fix my sandwich how I like it," he would say to her, without really knowing how that was. Others in their circle of friends asked Floyd for his vote of video or cocktail but they rarely waited for his answer. They simply doubled Rebecca's request. He seemed more and more like the Styrofoam man of Zelda's inflammatory remark. She had chosen him to maintain her freedom but instead had become the chief window dresser of his world, feeding and clothing and positioning him while he became paler, more passive, more lifeless. Rebecca cast into the water with an angry flick of her wrist. His passivity was also her loss, as more and more of her went into infusing him with the life that he should have had for himself. Being in control of Floyd's life simply meant that Floyd's life was in control of her own.

Standing next to her, Zelda reeled in a walleye, hooting with pleasure.

"We're the one's who've died and gone to heaven, honey," Zelda said. "This is a season full a' fish!"

Rebecca turned back toward her house. "They're sending out the flotilla, Zelda." She gestured toward the sheriff's boat that had been set into the water.

Zelda hooked her spinner to the rod and held it like a staff. "Welcome to the widow's club, honey."

Rebecca turned away, and cast again.

CONTRIBUTORS' NOTES

Jennifer Armstrong has spent her life telling stories and making music with fiddle, banjo, bagpipe and words. Her autobiographical show *WomanSong* was produced by Northlight Theatre in 1995. Jennifer currently tours with her diverse programs of *Song Spun Stories* to a wide variety of audiences across the country.

Wendy Bashant is an Associate Professor of English at Coe College. Her poems have appeared in various anthologies and poetry magazines, as have her articles on nineteenth-century British literature and opera.

Mary Ber teaches English at Roosevelt University, publishes and edits the literary magazine *Moon Journal*, and is completing a Masters Degree in Women's Studies. She has published poems, short stories, and essays and has lived most of her life in the Chicago area.

Deanna Blackwell is a graduate student in African Studies at the University of Illinois at Urbana-Champaign. She remembers a sense of alienation that lingered as she moved from Springfield to Charleston, and then to Urbana, and her work reflects the friction of growing up a Black woman in a predominantly white Midwestern community. Her poetry has appeared in various local publications, the *Southern African Feminist Review*, and in a Chicago area photographic project.

Gayle Brandeis is a writer and dancer, a Chicago native now living in California. Her work has appeared in numerous magazines and anthologies, and has received several honors, including the 1998 Quality Paperback Book Club/Story Magazine Short Fiction Award. She has two books forthcoming: *Fruitflesh: Living and Writing in a Woman's Body*, and *Towards a Center of Voices: Women Poets on Women Poets and the Poetic Process.*

Patricia Cronin writes poetry. and short fiction, which has appeared in numerous journals. She is in the MFA Creative Writing Program at Roosevelt University in Chicago.

Victoria Dal Compo lives with her family in Algonquin, Illinois, and attends Jacobs High School in Lake in the Hills.

Ann Darr, born in Bagley, Iowa, wrote radio scripts and flew with the Women's Airforce Service Pilots (WASP) during World War II. She now teaches at The American University in Washington, D.C., and the Writers Center in Maryland. Her eight books of poetry include *Flying the Zuni Mountains*. She edited an anthology, *Hungry As We Are*. Her honors include an NEA fellowship, McDowell and Yaddo residencies, and Bunting Year at Radcliffe.

Scotty Denhollem, a mother of two, spent ten memorable years in the Midwest at graduate school in Indiana, law school in Illinois, and a six-year stint for the Associated Press in Chicago. Currently, she teaches Law Studies and English at a public high school in Shreveport, Lousiana.

Betty Diamond, who teaches at the University of Wisconsin-Whitewater, has published her plays most recently in *The Dramatists Guild Quarterly* and *Rosebud*. Her work has been seen in New York City, Chicago, and Madison, Wisconsin.

Laura Distelheim's writing has appeared in *An Intricate Weave: Women Write on Girls and Girlhood* (Iris Editions, 1997), and is forthcoming in *The Leap Years: Women Reflect on Change, Loss, and Love* (Beacon Press). In 1997, she received a grant from the Money for Women/Barbara Deming Memorial Fund for *Grace Notes*, her collection of literary essays in progress. In 1998, she received the Richard J. Margolis Award.

Rochelle Distelheim's fiction has been published in a number of literary journals, as well as in the anthologies *An Intricate Weave: Women Writing About Girls and Girlhood*, and *West Side Stories*. She is the recipient of the Katherine Ann Porter Prize in Fiction, Illinois Arts Council Fellowships in Fiction and Literary Awards, and several Pushcart Prize nominations.

Barbara Esstman was born in Carroll, Iowa, and grew up in St. Charles, Missouri. She is an NEA fellow and a *Redbook* fiction winner. Her two novels, The *Other Anna* and *Night Ride Home*, were both adapted for films by Hallmark Production. She is co-editor of *A More Perfect Union: Poems and Stories About the Modern Wedding* from St. Martin's Press.

Morgan Baylog Finn, a native Ohioan, lives in Connecticut. Her poem, "The Fruit Cellar," was dramatized as a video for Connecticut Public Television. She is currently at work on a novel, *The $2000 House*, set in Ohio.

Susan Firer has three published books: *The Lives of the Saints and Everything, The Underground Communion Rail*, and *My Life with the Tsar and Other Poems. The Lives of the Saints* won the Cleveland State University Poetry Prize and the Posner Award for the best book of poems published by a Wisconsin author in 1993.

Alice Friman, born in New York City, is professor emerita of English and creative writing at the University of Indianapolis where she has lived for forty years. Published in ten countries and anthologized widely, she has produced eight collections of poetry, including *Inverted Fire* (BkMk Press, 1997) and *Zoo*, forthcoming from the University of Arkansas Press. Among her numerous honors are three prizes from the Poetry Society of America, a fellowship from the Indiana Arts Commission, and the Ezra Pound Poetry Award for *Zoo*.

M. Eliza Hamilton Abégúndé was born in New Jersey and lived with her grandmother in Grenada, West Indies, before settling in the Chicago area. Her work has appeared in several magazines and anthologies, including *I Feel a Little Jumpy Around You, Catch the Fire*, and *Beyond the Frontier*. She is the author of two chapbooks, *What is Now Unanswerable* and *Still Breathing*, a member of the Blue Ellipsis Writer's Collective, a Reiki Master, tarot reader, dream-worker and daughter of Osun.

Wendy Heller moved from Philadelphia to Chicago in her early twenties. She is now an Associate Professor in clinical psychology at the University of Illinois, where she does research on brain function and non-verbal experience. She has previously published poems in the University of Pennsylvania Press and the Penn-Knox Press, and won a University of Chicago prize for her poem "Spartan Jar," which appeared in *Jane's Stories I* from Wild Dove.

Ridgely Jackson was born and spent her childhood in the same Northwest suburb of Chicago where she lives today with her son. For 25 years in between, she lived in San Francisco. Now she studies English and writing at Northwestern University, where she recently published her first story in the literary journal, *Helicon.* She feels there's much to be said for blooming slowly and late.

Danice Kern's award-winning career as a television reporter and producer has taken her on assignment around the world. Recently, she resigned from a senior news management position at a network-owned television station to teach and concentrate on her writing. She is the author of the novel, *Lake Time*, and of a poetry chapbook, *Boiled Molecules,* published by Wild Dove. Currently, she is at work on her second novel and another volume of poetry.

Patrice Clark Koelsch attended Ohio State University and now lives in Minnesota. Her work has appeared in *The Women's Review of Books, Art Papers,* as well as *The Hungry Mind Review.* She has been a writer in residence at Ragdale.

Marilyn Krysl's work has appeared in *O. Henry Prize Stories* and the *Pushcart Prize Anthology*. She won *Negative Capability*'s Fiction Award and *Spoon River Poetry Review*'s Award for Poetry. She received an NEA grant and a Yaddo residency, and directs the Creative Writing Program at the University of Colorado, Boulder, while co-editing the journal, *Many Mountains Moving.*

Sandra Sidman Larson served as executive director of two nonprofit organizations and raised three sons before she began writing seriously at 50. She has studied at the University of Minnesota and the Iowa Writers Workshop. She was nominated for a 1997 Pushcart Prize and is included in the 1999 anthology, *The New World,* edited by Naomi Shihab Nye.

Diane Lutovich is a partner in a training and consulting business by day and a poet by night. She is a former co-president of the Marin Poetry Center and has been published in many journals.

Marjorie Maddox is from Ohio and now teaches at Lock Haven University. Her first book, *Perpendicular As I*, won the Sandstone Publishing National Poetry Book award. Her two chapbooks, *Nightrider to Edinburgh* and *How to Fit God into A Poem*, also won awards. She has twice been nominated for the Pushcart Prize.

Marianne Marchese grew up in Nebraska, also living in Kansas and Missouri. She worked with the Chicago Dramatist Workshop and now works in Portland, Oregon with Stark Raving Theatre.

Shirley Vogler Meister was born in Illinois but has lived in Indiana for 40 years. A former editor for an Illinois daily, she worked at two national magazines, but now concentrates on freelancing. She has earned many awards, including one from the National League of American Pen Women. Her poems appear in several anthologies. Her sonnet, previously published in *When I am An Old Woman I Shall Wear Purple* by Papier-Mache Press,. was set to music by Chicago composer Brad Cresswell, and has been performed at Carnegie Hall and elsewhere by soprano Elizabeth

Futral..

Catherine Mellett's work has appeared in many journals and in the Papier-Mache anthology, *Generation to Generation.* She received a state Arts Council grant, the Monticello Fiction Fellowship at Villa Montalvo, and residencies at Ragdale and Yaddo.

Linda Mitchell has lived in Lake County or in other parts of the Chicago area most of her life. Her poems appeared in the chapbook *Wild Content*, from Wild Dove. She is also a musician, songwriter, and metalsmith.

Julie Moulds lives in Michigan. She received her MFA in Creative Writing from Western Michigan University, where she taught. In 1998, her first poetry book, *The Woman with A Cubed Head,* was published. An excerpt from her cancer journals is forthcoming in a Beacon Press anthology.

Andrea Potos is a Madison, Wisconsin bookseller at A Room of One's Own Feminist Bookstore. Her poems can be found in many journals; in the anthologies *I Feel a Little Jumpy Around You*, *Claiming the Spirit Within*, and *At Our Core: Women Writing About Power*; and in a chapbook of her poems, *The Perfect Day,* published by Parallel Press.

Jill Riddell teaches creative writing at the School of the Art Institute of Chicago and is the author of *The Big Middle*, an interactive novel that appeared on the Spiegel catalogue company's web site (1996-97). She writes nonfiction for *Chicago* and *Garden Design* magazines, the *Chicago Tribune*, and other publications, was a columnist for the Chicago *Reader* from 1994-96, and contributes essays and commentary to WBEZ, Chicago's public radio station. She received Audubon's award for excellence in environmental reporting in 1994 .

Jude Rittenhouse, born in Missouri and raised in Ohio, was once a resident of Illinois and now resides in Rhode Island. She received a Vermont Studio Writer's Grant. Her work has been in many journals and anthologies; she is a Contributing Editor for *Moon Journal.*

Sue Scavo was born and raised in Ohio, receiving a B.A. in English Literature from the University of Cincinnati. She now lives in rural Vermont.

Terry Lee Schifferns lives in a cabin on the south bank of the Platte River with her children and teaches writing at Central Community College in Grand Island, Nebraska. She has previously published work in journals and her writing is included in the '96 *We'Moon: Gaia Rhythms for Women* calendar and in *Against the Wind: Women Write from the Heart of the West.*

Tamara Sellman lived 12 years in the Chicago suburbs before recently reclaiming her roots in Washington state. She is the "Market Mosaic" columnist for *Wild Dove Review.*. Her work has appeared in a number of journals, and one of her stories was recently nominated for the Pushcart Prize. Another won a Best of Entry award from *Whelk's Walk Review.*

Shobha Sharma came to the United States from India. After raising two sons and working in the pharmaceutical industry, she began teaching English as a Second Language to immigrants from Central and South America. Presently, she is director of a parent program and works with several Chicago public schools. Her short stories have been published in several journals.

Deborah Shouse lives in Kansas. Her work has been published in *Ms., Woman's Day*, and *Reader's Digest.* She is the co-author of *Antiquing for Dummies.*

Shoshauna Shy was born and raised in Illinois, but now lives in Madison, Wisconsin. Her poems have been published recently in various journals and literary magazines, including the *Wisconsin Poets' Calendar: 1998* (and 1999) and *Double-Entendre.*, among others

Christine Swanberg has published several collections of poetry, including *Tonight on This Late Road* and *Invisible String* (Erie Street); *The Tenderness of Memory* (Plainview Press); *Bread Upon the Waters* (Windfall Prophets, University of Wisconsin, Whitewater) and *Where the Enchanted Live* (an artists' collaboration/handmade). She is a co-editor of *Korone* and founder of the Rock River Poetry Prize.

Cinda Thompson is a native of Southern Illinois and now lives in Peoria. A past rich in coal-mining history, as well as "rowdy" political roots, inform her work as does an interest in the lives of women. She has received several awards and grants for her work, and she is published in numerous anthologies and journals, including several by Papier-Mache Press, *Downstate Story, Korone*, as well as *Jane's Stories: An Anthology of Work by Midwestern Women* (*Jane's Stories I.*)

Bonnie Tunick's prose poems, vignettes, and photographs appeared in *Jane's Stories I* and in *The Lines in Her Face*, both from Wild Dove. She lives in Chicago and is Executive Director of the Fairy Godmother Foundation, which grants wishes to the terminally ill. Currently, she is seeking an agent for two completed novels.

Roz Warren has edited twenty collections of women's humor, including the classics *Women's Glib* and *Men Are From Detroit, Women Are From Paris.* She *is* from Detroit, but now lives in Pennsylvania.

Jess Wells' eight volumes of work include *Lesbians Raising Sons*, a Lambda Literary Award finalist, and the novel, *Aftershocks*, nominated for the American Library Association Gay and Lesbian Literary Award. In addition, she has published work in more than twenty anthologies, including *Queer View Mirror I & II, Tangled Sheets, Women on Women, Lavender Mansions, Lesbian Culture*, and *When I am An Old Woman I Shall Wear Purple.* Her four collections of short stories include *Two Willow Chairs*, and *The Dress/The Sharda Stories.* Look for her new collection, *Loon Lake Duet*, which will include "Women Who Fish."

Y. Regina "Bonnie" Whitmore was born and raised on the South Side of Chicago. Her poetry chapbook, *My Colors...and the Rainbow*, was published in 1997 by Wild Dove. Her passions for color and handiwork are employed in crafts from decorated cigar boxes to miniature dollhouses. She is a neurosurgical nurse at a Chicago hospital.

PERMISSIONS AND OTHER NOTES

The following works appeared first in other publications and are reprinted by permission:

Ann Darr, "The Bagley Iowa Poem," in *The Myth of a Woman's Fist;* Catherine Mellett, "On the Way to The Rink" in *Calliope* 1998; Shirley Vogler Meister, "Harvest" in *Grow Old Along with Me—The Best is Yet to Be*, Papier-Mache Press; Julie Moulds, "Renoir's Bathers" in *Architrave*, 1998; Patricia Cronin, "Maemal's Heart" in *Alabama Literary Review*; Rochelle Distelheim, "Home Movies" in *McCall's Magazine* and *An Intricate Weave: Women Writing About Girls and Girlhood*, Iris Editions, 1996; Laura Distelheim, "On Nina, Nightingales, and Surviving the Night" also appeared in *An Intricate Weave*; Jill Riddell, "Infinity Unplugged" in the *Chicago Reader*, April, 1995 (in an earlier version); Mary Ber, "Grief in Season #43" in *Moon Journal*, Spring/Summer 1997, Volume II, Issue I; Sue Scavo, an earlier version of "On My Religious Upbringing" in *Spillway*; Alice Friman, "Letter to the Children" in *Poetry Review (UK)*; "Telling Tales" in *Arts Indiana*; Morgan Baylog Finn, "Farmer's Wife in Defense of Their Runaway Tractor" in *Sunrust*, 1990; Jude Rittenhouse, "Snake Hands" in *Moon Journal,* Fall/Winter 1997; "Ella's Dakota Quilt" the Spring/Summer 1998 issue of the same journal; Christine Swanberg, "For Lee, Who Shoes Horses" in *Rockford Review*; Marilyn Krysl, "Dirt" in *High Plains Literary Review*; Roz Warren, "Auto Repair" in *Seventeen* Magazine; Danice Kern, "Boiled Molecules" and "Before the Poetry" in *Boiled Molecules*; Linda Mitchell, "Be Wild!" and "Keynote Speaker" in *Wild Content*; Y. Regina Whitmore, "Work of Art" in *My Colors...and a Rainbow*; the last three publications are chapbooks from Wild Dove Studio and Press, Inc.

<u>Editor's Note</u> The following products are registered trademarks of the indicated companies: Lifesavers and Now and Later, Nabisco Brands Company; Count Chocula and Lucky Charms, General Mills, Inc; Carnation, Everlasting Gobstopper, Nestle's, Nestle Crunch, The Nestle Company, Inc./Societe Des Produits Nestle S.A.; Pop Rocks, Kraft General Foods Inc.; Popsicles, Popsicle Industries Inc. dba Gold Bond-Good Humor Ice Cream; Handi Wipe, Colgate-Palmolive Company; Tab, The Coca-Cola Company.

THE WILD DOVE VISION

The vision to publish an anthology of writing by feminist regional writers began in 1994 with *Jane's Stories: An Anthology of Work by Midwestern Women* (now called informally *Jane's Stories I*). *Jane's Stories II* is a continuation of that vision. As we have learned more about the universe of book publishing, our view has widened to encompass nearer horizons. We now also provide workshops, retreats, editorial services, and a newsletter, all of which support one of our primary goals: to build community among women writers.

Interestingly, we have found that even those who have been frequently published often see only fragments of the industry. In the crazy-quilt world of publishing, our goal is to piece together a more wholistic viewpoint. In this way, writers will have more influence over the future direction of publishing.

Through the *Wild Dove Review* newsletter, we share what we know with other writers, so that we build a common knowledge base about how to publish and how to build an audience for our work. Our workshops, retreats, and other events are designed to maximize the opportunities of women writers to learn and to share new skills. Our readings help to develop a more general readership that seeks out and supports similar work.

Nothing is so encouraging as a circle of familiar faces at a reading, unless it be a more seasoned author sharing insights with an emerging talent.

We invite writers and readers everywhere to join us in this adventure. Whether you subscribe to our newsletter, attend our workshops or other events, attend our readings, or simply watch for our books in your bookstore or library, please let us hear from you.

Take a moment to look at the next few pages and see what we have to offer.

Available from Wild Dove

The **Wild Dove Review** includes, among other items of interest to writers and readers, articles about women writers, news from the publishing industry, and Tamara Sellman's Market Mosaic columns, which review literary journals from the viewpoint of writers seeking publication. Subscribe (only $10 per year for four issues!) by checking the box and filling in your name and shipping address below.

Jane's Stories: In Anthology of Work by Midwestern Women, (Jane I) edited by Glenda Bailey-Mershon, Clara Johnson, Linda Mowry, and Julie Sass. Thirty-one Midwestern authors and artists provide inspiration and entertainment.
ISBN 0-9639894-0-5 132 pp. $ 11 postpaid.

The Lines in Her Face: Inspiration and Snapshots from Bonnie Ilyse Tunick. No one else sees the world quite the way Bonnie does. Share her warm, tender, and often hilarious look at the lives and courage of "ordinary" women like the ones you know, or wish you did.
ISBN 0-9639894-8-0 52 pp $11 postpaid.

QTY	TITLE	$ EACH	TOTAL
	JANE'S STORIES II		
	JANE'S STORIESI (ORIGINAL)		
	THE LINES IN HER FACE		
	MY COLORS...AND A RAINBOW		
	WILD CONENT		
	BOILED MOLECULES		
	BIRD TALK		
	TOTAL		

PAYMENT METHOD: Check ❑ Money order ❑
(Payable to Wild Dove Studio and Press, Inc., P.O. Box 789, Palatine, IL 60078-0789) Visa ❑ Mastercard ❑
Account # ______________________________ Exp. date _________

Signature ____

Ship to: ____

____
Yes,I'd like to subscribe to the Wild Dove Review ($10) ❑

The **Midwest Women Poets Series** offers chapbooks from promising poets whose work offers unique visions. The chapbooks are also extraordinary in design, befitting the striking variety of the poetry.

My Colors... and a Rainbow by Y. Regina (Bonnie) Whitmore. This chapbook bursts with color from the hand-colored endpapers to the transcendent poetry. Poems about triumph and anguish from a caregiver who works with the desperately ill.
ISBN 1-891476-08-4 $8 postpaid

Wild Content by Linda Mitchell. Mitchell is a virtuoso of jazz and imagery who will send you flying like a kite, or underground to watch the secret life of spring-to-come. Colored like the Earth.
ISBN 1-891-476-06-8 $8 postpaid

Boiled Molecules by Danice Kern. Exquisite imagery and precise language from a noted journalist, emerging poet, and **Jane's Stories II** contributor. Gold-lettered cover.
ISBN 1-891476-01-7 $8 postpaid.

Bird Talk by Wild Dove founder Glenda Bailey-Mershon. Poems that seek the bridge between place and identity, between pushing off and letting go. Textured cover and a birdlover's design elements.
ISBN 1-891476-11-4 $8 postpaid

Two things readers can do to help support women writers:
1) Attend readings of their work.
2) Ask for their work by title in your favorite bookstore or library.
3) Let us hear from you! (See address at left.)
And look for our site coming soon on the World Wide Web!